Royal Priesthood

A series of studies on the priesthood of the believer

Ken Chant

Royal Priesthood

A Series of Studies on
The Priesthood of The Believer

By Ken Chant

ISBN 978-1-61529-072-7

Vision Publishing

1672 Main St. E 109

Ramona, CA 92065

1-800-9-VISION

www.booksbyvision.com

Table of Contents

DAZZLING TRUTH

My wife thinks I should not start my book with John Donne's 16th century poem, and she is probably right. Undoubtedly the metaphysical Donne does have a soporific, or at best bewildering effect upon many readers. You may think he deserves the satirical description -

" ... pensive poets painful vigils keep,
Sleepless themselves to give their readers sleep.[1] "

Yet he remains my favourite poet, and the following lines from his satire **Kind Pity** wonderfully set the right frame of mind for the study of an exalted theme. If poetry wearies you, then skip ahead to my next paragraph. But you may find it worth the effort to meditate on the poet's wisdom. My endnotes will help you to catch the meaning of his closely packed ideas -

Careless Phrygius[A] doth abhor
All, because all cannot be good, as one
Knowing some women whores, dares marry none.
Gracchus[B] loves all as one, and thinks that so
As women do in divers countries go
In divers habits, yet are still one kind,
So doth, so is religion; and this blindness
too much light breeds[C]; but unmoved thou
Of force must one, and forced but one allow[D];
And the right; ask thy father which is she[E],
Let him ask his ...

... On a huge hill,
Cragged and deep, Truth stands, and he that will
Reach her, about must, and about must go;
And what the hill's suddenness resists, win so;[F]
Yet strive so, that before age, death's twilight,
Thy soul rest, for none can work in that night[G].
To will, implies delay, therefore now do[H].

---

[1] Alexander Pope (1688-1744), **The Dunciad**, Book One, lines 93,94

Hard deeds, the body's pains;[1] hard knowledge too
The mind's endeavours reach,and mysteries
Are like the sun, dazzling, yet plain to all eyes.

Some truth, as the poet said, is like the sun, too dazzling to penetrate; some mysteries are too fathomless to plumb. Yet their very brilliance compels every looking eye to see them. So is the doctrine that occupies the pages of this book: the splendid and pivotal truth of **the priesthood of every believer**. It is perhaps the most important doctrine in the New Testament, and certainly the most revolutionary. Yet it has this anomaly: although it stands plainly written on every page of the gospel it remains one of the most difficult truths to penetrate. That is because it defies the common ideas most people have about religion, and it calls for a breathtaking boldness of faith in approaching the throne of God.

Yet just as **"hard deeds are done through bodily pain"** so, if you apply your mind and soul to scripture, giving your best **"endeavour"** to gaining an inner revelation of the word of God, you will surely emerge transformed by recognition of the **royal priesthood** God has given you in Christ.

A word more. Because of its hardness, this doctrine has aroused many rending quarrels in the church. I cannot avoid taking a side in the argument; but I hope to do so with grace, following the generous and worthy example of Sir Thomas Browne-

"I could never divide myself from any man upon the difference of an opinion, or be angry with his judgment for not agreeing with me in that from which perhaps within a few days I should dissent myself. I have no Genius to disputes in Religion, and have often thought it wisdom to decline them, especially upon a disadvantage, or when the cause of truth might suffer from the weakness of my patronage. ... Every man is not a proper Champion for Truth, nor fit to take up the Gauntlet in the cause of Verity. Many, from the ignorance of these Maxims, and from an inconsiderate zeal unto Truth, have too rashly charged the troops of error, and remain as Trophies unto the enemies of Truth. A man may be in as just possession of Truth as of a City, and yet be forced to surrender. 'Tis therefore better to enjoy her with peace, than to hazard her upon a battle."[2]

I feel the weight of the good physician's words: "I have no Genius to disputes in Religion, and have often thought it wisdom to decline them especially ... when the cause of truth might suffer from the weakness of my patronage." I am perhaps more willing to throw myself into the fray than Browne was, and he might therefore wish to number me among those who "too rashly charge the troops of error". Nonetheless, I do feel the inadequacy of my resources. So I must leave you to judge for yourself whether my patronage of the **royal priesthood** has enhanced or hindered your proper understanding of its splendour.

At least I hope that our Great High Priest is not too displeased with my efforts, and may perhaps even approve them.

End Notes

A. Because a succession of conquerors had imposed upon them so many different religions the Phrygians were renowned for scorning them all.

B. The Gracchi were a Roman patrician family who flourished during the 2nd century B.C. They were famous for their liberal philosophy, and their willingness to tolerate and respect a wide variety of opinions on morals, religion, and philosophy.

C. Those who are too willing to see truth in every religious dogma, or to allow that there is value in every creed, will be blinded by an excess of light.

D. Of necessity, only one religion can be true; therefore even under duress that religion, and that alone, must be proclaimed as truth.

E. Before anyone can threaten you with violence, make sure you have settled upon the right religion. How can you be sure? Ask your

---

[2] "Religio Medici" Part One, Sec. 6; Penguin Classics edition, 1977; ed. C. A. Patrides; pg. 65. I have slightly modified the original spelling and punctuation. Sir Thomas Browne was an English physician of extraordinary learning and benign character. His book ("The Religion of a Doctor") was first published in 1643, and has never since been out of print.

father's father - that is, go back to the original gospel, and to the apostles.

F. The sensible way to climb to the top of a steep hill is to work your way around it, not try to go straight up. So truth must be won by patient and comprehensive study.

G. Give yourself to study while you are young, before old age makes such toil too wearisome.

H. Good intentions are not enough; they may just lead to endless delay. Start now in your quest for truth

I. Just as great deeds require physical exertion, and nothing worthwhile is done without pain, so knowledge is gained by hard mental endeavour.

Chapter One:

DRAW NEAR TO GOD

Greek mytholngy tells the story of the fifty daughters of Danaus, who were called the *Danaids*. Danaus was the king of Argos, and he was at war with his brother Aegyptus, who had fifty sons. The young men gathered an army, laid siege to Argos, and overcame it. Among the terms of surrender demanded by Aegyptus was a pact for Danaus to give his fifty daughters in marriage to their cousins. The night for the wedding celebration was fixed, the festivities began, and the people rejoiced, believing that the union of the two families would bring peace to them all. But bitter in defeat, Danaus instructed each of his daughters to conceal a long pin in her hair and on the wedding night to plunge it deep into the heart of her groom. This was done, and in one night all fifty of the young men perished. The Danaids and their father were delighted by the triumph; but (says the myth) the gods of Olympus were not pleased. The Danaids were called into judgment and a terrible doom passed upon them: they were condemned forever to carry water in jars perforated with many holes!

That scene of the despairing maidens endlessly repeating their futile task became a favourite of many artists. They saw in it a metaphor of the frustration of ordinary life - the dreary round of repetitive actions, seemingly without purpose; the mindless fluctuations of fortune; the treadmill of remorseless destiny that many people feel has imprisoned them.

Is that how you feel about yourself? Do you feel condemned to a fate as remorseless as the mythical one suffered by the Danaids. Do your days seem empty of hope, possessing no purpose beyond the grave, no destiny past death, locked into a monstrous cycle of futility? Is life a dreary succession of vain struggles, like carrying water in buckets without bottoms?

How stunningly the Bible reverses that bleak prospect! In our hopelessness we turn to scripture and at once find boundless hope! Consider for example this passage:

"Let us come boldly to the throne of grace and there receive mercy and find grace to help us in our time of need." (He 4:16)

Here is a promise of limitless access and limitless help; here is a declaration of the astonishing privileges God has given to every person who truly believes in Christ.

The apostle expresses it in five stunning invitations -

COME TO THE THRONE

We can hardly imagine how revolutionary this invitation seemed to the people who first heard it. The idea that ordinary people could freely approach the Lord God of all heaven and earth was quite incredible to them. Their first instinct was to reject it with scornful disbelief - much as you would do if you heard that the doors of Buckingham palace were being thrown open to all and sundry. Imagine anyone who had a fancy for it wandering in at any time, sauntering up to the throne, sitting on it, and chatting with the Queen! Even if you saw such an invitation printed in the newspapers you would not believe it. You really could not imagine the way to the throne being so open.

If you have you ever stood with the crowd, pressing your nose between the wrought iron bars of the fence around the palace, watching the Changing of the Guard, then you know how unlikely such an open-house policy would be. Warriors everywhere! Anyone foolish enough to amble through the splendid gates, and across the quadrangle toward the massive doors of the palace, could expect swift arrest and expulsion!

Alison and I were once invited to a royal garden party and had an opportunity to meet briefly with the Queen and Prince Philip. But the number of guests was strictly limited, and we ourselves were invited only once. Then, some years later, when we were in London, we did stand with mobs of tourists gawking through the fence railings at the troops marching back and forth. Although the great iron gates to the palace grounds and the splendid palace doors all stood enticingly open, we dared not walk through them. One invitation to a garden party gave us no access to the throne! We remained banished to the outer fence!

So the ancients thought about God. He is a Mighty Lord. He is a Great King. Only the most noble had unhindered access to this throne. They deemed it unthinkable that common people could speak with him whenever they pleased. So the assertion that anyone could come to the throne of God whenever they wanted to was startling. No one had ever dared to imagine that such an open path to the heavenlies was even possible, let alone actually existed.

But surely religion had opened the way to God? Did not the priests in the various temples and shrines of the Greeks and Romans encourage the people to pray, and to draw near to whichever deity they worshipped? The answer, in fact, is "NO!" Why? Because across the entire span of human history, the purpose of religion has never been to bring people *to* God, but rather to keep them *away* from him!

Religion found its very origin in that purpose. A people aware of their own sin and of heaven's holiness, in terror of divine judgment, chose some men to be priests, and commanded them to create whatever religious structure was necessary to create a safe barrier between earth's fault and heaven's fury.

So religion has always existed solely to protect people from getting too close to a god who would surely destroy them in a moment were they to profane him by their presence. All the apparatus of religion across the centuries - the altars, sacrifices, ceremonies, priesthoods, temples, and the like were designed with one purpose: to keep the god safely in heaven, where he belonged, and to allow the people to keep their distance while they got on with their lives. Bringing God and man together was not the religious task; rather, it was to keep them as far apart as possible!

So here were two absolute opposites: the ancient faiths, which we could summarise as the *religion of barriers*; and the new faith of Christ, the *gospel of invitation*.

THE RELIGION OF BARRIERS

Despite what you may have thought, even the religion God established in Israel by the hand of Moses was not intended to open a path between heaven and earth, but to place as many protective barriers as possible between a fallen nation and their infinitely holy Deity.

The Hebrews lived in dread of any personal encounter with Yahweh - see *Jg 6:22-23; Ex 19:12-13; 20:18-21*; plus many similar references. When Moses built his tabernacle in the wilderness, and Solomon the temple in Jerusalem, the controlling principle was that of keeping the people distant from God. That rule remained unchanged for centuries and still governed Israel's religious life when the letter to the Hebrews was written. Even as the apostle gave the invitation, "come to the throne," the temple was still standing in Jerusalem, with wall after wall barricading the holy place from the surrounding city.

Thus from the very beginning the people were fenced off from God. When the law was being given to Moses they were forbidden to set foot even on the base of the mountain -

> *"You have not been brought to a mountain you can touch, like Sinai, with its blazing flames, its gloomy darkness, its howling winds, its clamorous trumpet, its thunderous voice. When the people heard the sound, they begged the voice to speak no more, for they could not endure its dread command: `Whatever creature sets foot upon the mountain must be stoned to death.' The light was so appalling that even Moses cried out, `I am shaking with terror!" (He 12:18- 21; Ex 19:10ff)*

Thus their religion began, and thus it continued. Consider the vast temple that still stood in Jerusalem when the gospel was first preached. It was surrounded by a high wall that created a spacious area known as the "Court of the Gentiles". This Court was open to all worshippers. But as you crossed it, you came to a barrier and a gate, with a notice threatening death to any gentile who walked into the "Court of the Women". Into that Court only ceremonially clean Jewish men and women could enter.

If you crossed the "Court of the Women", you came to another barrier and a gate, which led into the "Court of the Israelites". There too was a notice, threatening death to any woman who attempted to go through it. It was open only to ceremonially clean Jewish men.

At the far end of that court (in which were placed the altar of sacrifice and the great brass laver) stood the temple proper, with its two compartments: the "Holy Place", and the "Holy of Holies".

The "Holy Place" contained the splendid gold candlestick with its many branches, the golden altar of incense, and the table of bread. Into it only ceremonially clean priests who were rostered for duty could enter, and even they only when the required rituals were properly fulfilled. Instant death was the penalty for unlawful entry.

Then came the "Holy of Holies", closed off by its massive curtain. There stood the "Ark of the covenant and the two golden cherubs. Here, upon pain of immediate death for violators, only the high priest was allowed to enter, and even he only once a year. There the "shekinah", the glory of God, was thought to dwell, shining with dazzling splendour between the downcast faces of the cherubs. So unendurable was the sight that the purest high priest, who had fully satisfied all ceremonial demands, dared not enter until first he had filled the place with a thick cloud of incense.

Then he would hasten in with averted eyes, quickly sprinkle the atoning blood on the mercy seat, and rush out again, lest he gaze a moment too long at the divine magnificence and be struck dead. In case this should happen, a silk cord was attached to his ankle with its free end passing under the heavy veil, so that his corpse could be dragged out of the holiest without any other priest having to brave the awful peril of going unlawfully behind the curtain.

So was Israel's sacred religion. Barrier upon barrier upon barrier standing between the people and the glorious presence of their God. To approach him was impossible.

Even to speak his name was deemed a fearful risk, so that by the time of Jesus no one dared pronounce the dread tetragrammaton "YHWH", and the sound of it had been forgotten. When the rabbis read the scriptures aloud they replaced "YHWH" with another and less perilous divine title, such as "Adonai" (Lord).

What was true of the Jewish religion in the time of Christ was true of the religions of all her gentile neighbours, and has remained true of religious dogma and practice everywhere in the world since then: religion does not exist to bring common people close to God, but to keep them as far away from him as possible.

Into that scene there suddenly sprang a new idea, startling, revolutionary, unlike anything that had ever before been spoken. It was:

THE GOSPEL OF INVITATION

"The way into the holiest is now open!" cried the apostles, "so let us come to the throne of God, and there meet with him face to face!"

No one had ever before dared to say such a thing. No one had ever before dared to make God so accessible to anyone who desired to approach him. What? Are there no barriers? Is there no ceremony? How can this be?

Whence came this open door? What is the source of this incredible invitation? Can I trust it without peril?

The apostles answered every protest -

> *"Dear friends, by the blood of Jesus we have now obtained full freedom to walk into the holy of holies itself. By the rending of his own body (which was like tearing down the great veil), he has opened up for us a new and living way. So then, let us draw near to God, coming with a sincere heart, unwavering confidence, sure faith, and cleansed inside and outside - that is, freed from a guilty conscience, and our bodies washed (as it were) with pure water. Stand firm and unyielding, holding fast to your confession of hope, for you can trust absolutely the Giver of the promise" (He 10:19-23).*

But if an open invitation to approach the throne of God was remarkable, even more astonishing was the next invitation:

COME BOLDLY TO THE THRONE

The apostle now puts an adverb into his invitation which must have made it even more amazing to the ancient world. In our day we are accustomed to friendly monarchies, where kings and queens walk down the street, conversing with, even shaking the hands of, ordinary people. Not so in Bible days. Then sovereigns lived in isolated and terrible majesty. To approach the king uninvited courted death. It was perhaps conceivable that a monarch might invite a commoner to approach his throne; but no one in Bible days would have imagined a commoner walking "boldly" into the royal presence and beginning a friendly chat with the king! Even the "high-born" were often required by oriental despots to crawl on their knees up to the throne, or to slither on their stomachs. They might also be obliged to kiss the tyrant's foot.

Remember the peril Esther placed herself when she appeared before her sovereign lord uninvited -

> *"Esther sent this message to her uncle Mordecai: `Please gather all the Jews who are in Susa, and beg them to fast and pray for me for three days and three nights. I and my maids will also fast and pray. After that, against the rules of the palace, I will enter the king's*

chamber, and if I die, then I shall die.' ... So on the third day Esther put on her finest robes, walked into the palace, across its inner court, and stood just outside the door of the throne room. The king, seated upon his royal throne, and facing the door, saw her. Happily, she gained his favour, so that he held out toward her his golden sceptre. She approached cautiously, and touched only its very tip" (Es 4:15- 5:2).

Because Esther was queen, she was permitted to walk up to the throne. Less exalted persons would have come with their heads deeply bowed, or on their knees, or even sliding prostrate, to kiss perhaps the monarch's finger, or more likely his foot. That is the way kings had been approached for centuries; that is the way they were still being approached in the time of Christ.

Hence Solomon, who was a true oriental despot, expressed the normal relationship between sovereign and subject, when he offered the advice -

"Don't take liberties when you go into the house of God. ... Don't speak impulsively; think before you open your mouth; choke back that rash promise. God is in heaven; you are on earth. So say as little as you can! Just as nightmares are caused by being too busy, so too many words will bring upon you a fool's miseries" (Ecc 5:1-3).

How astonishing then to hear the apostle say: "Let us come boldly to the throne of grace!"

He uses a striking word, which in the original Greek text is "parrhesia", a term coined from three other words that meant "all-words-say". The Greeks invented this word to describe the democratic right of free speech that belonged inalienably to every citizen of Athens. Whoever wanted to could stand up in the public assembly and say whatever was in his mind, without inhibition or threat of penalty - just as our politicians may say what they like when they speak in the House under "parliamentary privilege".

From this democratic freedom, "parrhesia" was extended by the Greeks to embrace boldness and confidence in general; but it never lost the idea of unrestrained liberty of speech, the right to say whatever you please, even in front of the highest authority, without restraint or fear.

Can we do this with God? Yes, for we are children, not slaves. We have freedom of speech in the Father's presence. There is no need to clothe ourselves with pious pretense, no value in mouthing religious platitudes, no use in disguising our true feelings. Say what is in your heart! Speak honestly before the Lord.

Tell him your joys and your sorrows, your hopes and your fears, your trust and your doubt, your virtues and your vices. Of course, he already knows it all. But you need to share your innermost thoughts with him. You have freedom to do so, in Christ.

But still someone might say: "Well, suppose I can come boldly to the throne, so what?

What can I hope to find there?"

The answer is found in the remainder of our text -

COME BOLDLY AND FIND MERCY

Few men have had such an enormous influence upon the world-wide church as St Thomas Aquinas, known as the "angelic doctor" - both because of his vast learning, and also because of the following story. From childhood Thomas was separated from his siblings and neighbours by the earnestness of his piety and the seriousness of his devotion to the scriptures. Instead of relinquishing these pursuits when he reached adolescence, he became ever more dedicated to prayer and study. His brothers, alarmed and thinking he was crazed, decided to distract him. So they brought a lovely maiden into his den and left her alone with him. But Thomas, with hot indignation, snatched a brand from the fire, scorched the sign of the cross on the chimney piece, and then, rushing at the girl drove her screaming from the room.

That much of the story is apparently true. I am not so sure about what follows. But we are told that God, mightily impressed by the young man's virtue sent two angels to reward him with a mystical girdle of chastity. Thereafter, he was free from all sensual temptation.

That was good fortune for St Thomas. Unhappily, the rest of us are not so lucky!

Temptation besets us all so easily, and sin is too often the consequence. Even if we are not guilty of any overt transgression of the laws of God, which of us has not sinned by falling short of the glory of God (Ro 3:23)

- like an arrow, which though aimed truly enough at the target, ever falls short of its mark? Has there ever been a moment in your entire life when you even once managed to act, speak, or think as nobly as you should have done? Sadly, your answer must be "no!" for we are incapable of reaching the divine glory in anything we do.

Therefore we need mercy. It is the first and last thing we need from God. It is the greatest thing we need. Without mercy there is nothing we can receive from the Father's hand; with mercy, there is nothing we cannot receive. But how great is that mercy? Is there a sin that can outreach it? Hardly! Tip a bottle of ink into the ocean. Will it darken the rolling seas? Can a leaf resist the buffeting gale? Can the black night swallow the glory of the new-rising sun? If you can blemish the world's waters with a few drops of dye, or catch a hurricane with a tissue, or make darkness stronger than light, then you will be able to swallow the mercy of God in your sin. Until then his mercy is always wider than your iniquity, and his grace higher than all your wrongdoing.

I do not mean that sin is inconsequential. Once having looked at the cross, and the Man who died there, how could anyone minimise the horror of sin? To overcome human corruption exhausted the life blood of the incarnate Christ. It cost God his own Son, and there can be no remission of our fault unless we allow faith to carry us into union with Christ. But to all who do believe in Jesus, the promise is sure, the most scarlet sin, the most crimson transgression, will be fully forgiven (Is 1:18- 20).

What is mercy? When the Lord shows us mercy, he is kindly disposed toward us and is willing to overlook the injuries we have done to him; he treats us with great forbearance, despite our many offences, and is very clement toward us though we deserve it not. In mercy he pardons us, in pleasure he restores us, in authority he cleanses us, in kindness he rewards us. How much we need his mercy! But his willingness to be merciful is always immensely greater than our need.

COME BOLDLY AND FIND GRACE

Grace: this is a word whose meaning is almost without boundaries. We may say that he is inviting us to come to the throne and

- find favour in the eyes of God
- find kindness from the hand of God

- find the means to be approved of God
- find dignity in the sight of God
- find strength to do the will of God
- find the desire to be agreeable to God
- find the friendship of God.

In finding grace, we find the free, unmerited love and favour of God; the strong influence of the Holy Spirit to renew our heart; a new ability to adore God and to turn our backs on sin. By grace we become reconciled to God, which enables the Lord to impart to us those characteristics of godliness as faith, meekness, humility, patience. If we find grace, we gain instruction, improvement, edification.

The grace of God is the favour of God. But what kind of favour? Favour is of many kinds -

- favour shown to the miserable - we call mercy
- favour shown to the poor - we call pity
- favour shown to the suffering - we call sympathy
- favour shown to the pig-headed - we call patience.

But when favour is shown to the unworthy, then we call it grace. It is privilege, pardon, prerogative, granted not by right, not when it is deserved, but solely by kind favour. When the Lord God shows us his grace, he raises us from debasement to dignity, from dishonour to honour, and places his own likeness within us. It is a sweet thing to find grace.

Notice that we "receive" mercy and "find" grace. The one carries the sense of instant possession, the other of gradual; the one is passive, the other is active. In a moment we may obtain, or get, mercy. But grace we find. It is like a buried treasure that we must dig for more and more. Mercy brings "forgiveness" of sin, full pardon; but by grace we are to overcome sin and to bear the likeness of God. Mercy we must simply accept; but grace we must experience. Mercy is given to us in a few words of forgiveness; but grace is an active thing that must work within us. We must search to find out the secret of grace, to comprehend the riches of grace, to discover the working of grace.

What is this grace? The Greek word is "charis", from which comes our word "charismatic". It describes the supernatural ability of God to work miracles, answer prayer, heal the sick, bring deliverance, and the like. By this grace, poverty is turned into prosperity, defeat into victory, and sin into righteousness. This grace moves mountains, hushes the turbulent seas, turns the impossible into the possible, and brings all of God's omnipotence into the arena of human need.

Sadly, many Christians are content to come to the throne of God and there only receive mercy; they never go on to find grace. Thus they experience only half of God's cure of sin. Rather, we should press on into the "double cure" described by the poet -

> "Rock of Ages, cleft for me,
> Let me hide myself in thee;
> Let the water and the blood
> From thy riven side which flowed,
> Be of sin the double cure,
> Cleanse me from its guilt and power!"[3]

Never be content to receive only mercy at the cross; do not be satisfied merely to be rid of sin's guilt. Resolve also to find the grace that will rescue you from its power. Then press forward to an ever richer and fuller possession of all that lies in the magnificent promise God has given us in Christ.

COME BOLDLY AND FIND HELP

So far in a remarkably colourful verse the apostle has used a political term (boldly), then a judicial one (mercy), then a theological (grace), and now a nautical term (help).

The Greek word is found only twice in the New Testament; here in our text; and in Ac 27:17, where we are told that the sailors "braced" their ship to prevent it from sinking and drowning all on board. The word comes from the time when men sailed the oceans in wooden ships. In English the equivalent nautical term is to "frap" a vessel. What does it mean?

---

[3] (A. M. Toplady, c. 1775)

Imagine a wooden sailing ship running into a furious storm. Under the awful pounding of the gale-driven waves, the planks of the ship begin to spring apart, allowing the sea to pour into the reeling vessel. Unless the gaps can be closed, the broken ship will soon fill with water and founder in the pitiless sea. What can be done?

One of the ways to save such a ship was to "frap" it by pulling ropes around its hull. The ropes were then fixed to a long bar, which was twisted like a windlass until the planks had been forced tightly together again. In a large ship, this might have to be done two or three times down its length.

How were the ropes carried around the ship? Usually a man would have to dive overboard, holding a cord in his teeth, swim under the ship and up the other side, then clamber aboard again so that his mates could use the cord to pull a heavier rope around the vessel.

Volunteers would be asked for, and many a brave seaman trying to save his ship instead lost his own life, carried away by the beating winds and waves. Some were driven against the keel and torn to pieces by the sharp barnacles and shells that encrusted its bottom. But some succeeded; and when the rope was carried around, and drawn tight, and the vessel successfully "frapped", then despair turned to joy.

Those who were dead were now alive again, confident they would safely reach their harbour.

That is the picture the apostle had in mind when he dipped into the language of the sea to say that we could flee to the throne of grace to find a "frapping" in our time of need!

He thinks of us as sailing through a savage gale, battered, waterlogged, in imminent peril of plunging forever beneath the pitiless waves. Is there no one who will offer to leap into the inky depths, braving a fearful death, to carry the needed lifeline up the other side? Yes! One is found! It is Jesus of Nazareth, who casts himself recklessly into the clawing waters of our sin and sickness, our weakness and poverty, our despair and death, and disappears from sight. Will he rise again? Surely the furious seas have imprisoned him forever? No! There he is! He stands on the decks victorious! The lifeline is in his hands! The sinking vessel can now be rescued and sail safely on to its pleasant harbour!

Perhaps even as you read these lines you are like that trembling ship. Your life is coming apart. The waves are pounding you to pieces. What can you do? How can you be saved? Just come boldly to the throne of grace. There in the midst of the storm call upon the Saviour. He waits with a miracle of answered prayer to 'frap' you, to pull you together, to meet your need, to make you whole, to set you safely on your way again!

TOO LITTLE TOO LATE?

There is a peculiarity in our text. The last phrase in Greek is ambiguous; it can be translated either, "help in time of need," or "help in good time." The idea in the second reading is that God is never too late, his help is always "timely". Sometimes it may not seem that way. Sometimes it does seem that God deals with us as the allies did with Germany earlier this century, always coming (as Allan Nevins said) with "too little too late". But we Christians are called to trust the Lord, to assert that he is never false to his word. If in your time of need it seems that the Lord has forsaken you, come back to his promise. Perhaps you did not turn to him when you should have done; perhaps you did not come boldly enough to his throne; perhaps you did not act strongly enough to seize his "helping grace"; or perhaps he helped you in a way different from the one you expected? This much I know;

"Come boldly to the throne of grace and you will surely find mercy and receive grace to give you timely help when you are in need!" So then:

- come boldly, without fear of sin because it is the throne of grace.

- come boldly, without fear of failure because it is the throne of his greatness.

- come boldly, without fear of Christ who rules there, because he is touched with the feeling of your infirmity.

- come boldly, without fear of the way being closed, because he is passed through the heavens.

- come boldly, without wavering, holding fast to your expectation of grace, mercy, and help from the generous hand of the Saviour.

Yet despite all that I have said, we still cannot approach the Throne of Grace unless one other thing is true of us: we must be priests. Why? Because of a principle that all religions - from the beginning of human history until now - have recognised: only priests have right of access to God. Shall we then find ourselves finally cut off from the

throne? Read on for the incredible answer!

Chapter Two:

ROYAL PRIESTS

Across the ages the great question has been: how can God convey his blessing to a fallen people? Were the Holy One to approach them, they would be consumed as the nearing flame shrivels paper.

"No mortal can ever see God, and live" (Ex 33:18-22).

Were they to approach God, they would perish like moths drawn to the dazzling flame. Our King is "eternal, immortal, invisible, dwelling in a realm of inaccessible splendour". No one has ever seen him. No one ever will see him" (1 Ti 1:17; 6:16).

Is there no way to bridge this awful chasm? Can this hiatus of darkness never be crossed? Humans cannot do it. Angels cannot do it. Perhaps even the wisdom of God will be baffled? So the cry was raised: must heaven and earth forever be cut off from each other? Will there never be a way to the throne?

Then God acted. He called for a Mediator to stand between the disgraced people and their offended Deity. Behind his advocacy, sinful people could present their requests to God; by his hand the Father's mercy and goodness could be channelled to the people. Who would respond to the call? Among all heaven's host, only One was adequate -

> *"I heard a majestic angel crying aloud, `Who is worthy ... ?' But no one could be found, neither in heaven, nor on earth, nor under the earth ... And because there was no one worthy, I began to weep bitterly. But one of the elders said to me, `Stop weeping, for the Lion of the tribe of Judah ... has won the battle.' Then I saw a Lamb standing (by the throne), still bearing the wounds of sacrifice, (and the heavenly host) began to sing a new song -*
>
>> *"You are worthy ... ,*
>> *For you were slain,*
>> *And by your blood you have obtained for God*
>> *people from every clan, tongue, nation and tribe,*

> *And you have made them a house of "royal*
> *priests"*
> *For the service of God;*
> *And they shall reign on the earth'"* (Re 5:1-10).

We notice a strange thing: it is not enough to have only a Mediator in heaven, Christ, the Lamb of God. Earthly mediators of the blessing of God are also required. Those whom Christ has purchased for God by his blood, are at once designated a "house of royal priests", who stand between the larger community and Christ, and become the channels through whom his saving grace is mediated to the world. If Christ is the *High Priest in Heaven*, then we are his Royal Priests on Earth.

What does that mean? What privileges are inherent in this title? What responsibilities does it entail?

Let us begin by observing the most startling aspect of the vision John saw: the entire company of redeemed people were called priests. The honour belonged to each one of them, not just to an ordained clergy nor to a separated group of officials. Do I mean that there is no room in the church for a distinct group of professional ministers? Hardly, since the writings of the apostles abound with references to various ministry functions, some of which require full-time commitment. How then can the people maintain their royal priesthood in the presence of a class of ordained and professional clergy?

To answer that question, we must first consider what is the church. Certain things have to come together before a group of people can be said (in the biblical meaning of the word) to constitute a true church. Where any of these factors are substantially absent, it must be doubted if that congregation deserves to be called a "church".

(1) The true gospel must be preached, proclaiming Christ as the sole source of pardon and eternal life.

(2) The Holy Spirit must be at work in and through that preaching, to produce a response in the hearers of genuine repentance and whole-hearted faith in Christ as the one sufficient Lord and Saviour.

(3) There must be an assembling together of those who have believed, in a visible expression of unity and faith. This congregation must meet regularly, in an organised way, and so demonstrate its coherence as the "Body of Christ" on earth. There are no private Christians in the New Testament. Every believer was part of a structured local church.

(4) Each local congregation must commit itself to an active fulfilment of the purposes of God, which are that -

(a) the church must be a company of people who have placed themselves unreservedly under his government, which means under the absolute lordship of Christ; and that

(b) the people must show their concern for each other by mutual fellowship and care, entering into a covenant relationship with each other in Christ; and that

(c) the people must be submissive to the disciplines of the church, expressed through

- the ministry of the word, teaching, exhorting, admonishing, rebuking, encouraging, strengthening, and shaping each hearer into the image of Christ

- the observance of the sacraments, which inspire repentance, faith, spiritual renewal, healing, and total consecration to Christ

- the practice of worship, recognising that there is indeed no church unless the preaching of the word has created faith, shown by a response of hearty praise and adoration toward God

- the doing of witness, carrying the light of the gospel into the dark world outside.

Out of the juncture of such things a local church is born. But then, out of this church arise various other functions: ministries, officers, servants, and the like; that is, pastors, elders, deacons, administrators, teachers, evangelists, and so on. These functions are all brought into being *by* the church; they do not create it; they are part of it, not separated from it; they are not above it, nor are they outside it, independent of it. If we could comprehend all such functions under the title of the "priesthood" then we would say, not that the priesthood creates the church, but that the church gives rise to the priesthood.

But scripture says that we are all *"royal priests"* in the calling of God. Therefore, the highest dignity of the priesthood, the *right* to minister the word and the sacraments, belongs to every Christian, even if in *practice,* that right will normally be restricted to those to whom the church itself gives the office.[4] So far as their right as Christians is concerned, every believer is fit and eligible for any office in the church. All are *priests*, not just those who belong to the ordained clergy. Thus the Greek word for "priest" (*hiereus*) occurs more than 30 times in the NT, but is not once used in an exclusive sense of a Christian minister.

We are all members of the one Body, serving the one Lord, sharing one Faith and one Baptism. Before the throne of God there is no distinction of race, sex, or class, for all have equal access to the holiest by the blood of Christ Ep 4:4-6; Ga 3:288; He 10:19-23). At once we encounter one of the arresting anomalies of the gospel. Christian life begins as a personal response to the word of God. We are drawn to the Cross, where sin is discretely dealt with, where repentance and faith are each an individual action. But no sooner have we stood *privately* in the presence of God, and become recipients of his gracious salvation, than we are instantly brought into a *collective* relationship with each other, as members of the vast community of faith. Being brought into the family, we cannot escape our duty to the brotherhood. We are made responsible for the family name, honour, and wellbeing. We are not free to abandon with impunity this duty.

Further, there is no higher status in the church than that of the royal priesthood, which honour every believer shares. Therefore, between Christians there exists no distinction of rank or value. If all are priests, if the highest echelon belongs to all, and the loftiest prestige, then lesser variations of office are insignificant. For convenience, we may talk about the "laity" and the "clergy", or about "people" and "pastor", but at the throne of God this is a distinction without a difference. It describes nothing more than a separation of tasks; it represents no shift in freedom to approach God, no diminishing of the believer's rights in Christ. Therefore one who is called (say) to be a carpenter has no less spiritual stature than one who is called to be a pastor. Neither of them holds any privilege in the heavenlies that is not equally and fully available to every other Christian.

---

[4] The particular place of the ordained clergy in the church, and the relationship of the various ministry functions to the royal priesthood is discussed in Chapters Three & Five.

See how plainly Paul described himself, without pomp, making no pretensions of superior prerogative -

> *"You should look on us simply as subordinates of Christ, the purveyors of God's hidden truth"* (1 Co 4:1)

Yet consider what grandiose authority Paul might have arrogated to himself, what claims he might have made.[5] But he knew well enough that whatever role he was given in the church added no value to him beyond what any other Christian possessed. They each had their own function in the church and in the world, as Paul had his; but in the presence of God they all stood equally tall, they all belonged to the same royal priesthood (Ph 3:4-9).

AARON OR MELCHIZEDEK

One reason why many Christians have restricted the concept (or else the practice) of the priesthood to a class of ordained officials, lies in the model they are following.

They base their ideas on the example of the Aaronic priesthood. There is much we can learn from Aaron and his descendants. Yet that was not the model upon which Christ based his ministry. Indeed, he largely ignored it. Rather, as the apostle tells us, he patterned himself upon an even more ancient example - that of Melchizedek. [6]Why did Christ reach so far back for his prototype? Why did he ignore the paradigm of priesthood that was well established in Israel and turn instead to the obscure Melchizedek?

First: because this had been predicted of him in scripture:

> *"Yahweh has sworn an oath. He will not alter his purpose. He declares: `You are a priest for ever, belonging to the order of Melchizedek.'"* (Ps 110:4)

Second: because the Jewish priesthood no longer functioned properly; the priests had become a privileged, wealthy, and powerful clique, and kept only the shell of true priesthood.

---

[5] See 2 Co 11:16 ff.; 12:10-11; etc

[6] Ge 14:18-20; Ps 110:4; He 5:6,10; 6:20; 7:1-17.

So Jesus turned to Melchizedek. Brief as the description is in Genesis, three things can be seen. Melchizedek was the king of Salem. He combined in himself the royal and priestly offices. He may also have held prophetic office, in which case he becomes a full type of Christ, who holds the threefold title of

Prophet - which shows that his government is *Spiritual*, not temporal;

Priest - which shows that his ministry is *Universal*, not local; and

King - which shows that his dominion is *Sovereign*, not subordinate to, as his "body" on earth possesses the same triple identity.

We are KINGS Born of the blood-royal, every Christian has a kingly identity. Our destiny is to reign with Christ -

> *"You are a royal priesthood ... He has fashioned us into a royal house, so that we might serve as priests of God ... You have made them into a company of royal priests ... They are priests of God and of Christ, and they will reign with him."* [7].

How could it be imagined that there is a more exalted position than this in the church? Do you believe in Jesus? Are you washed in the blood of the Lamb? Is Christ your Saviour and Lord? Then you have no lowly station! Call yourself no mere baron, nor count, nor earl, nor marquis, nor even duke. [8]Call yourself rather a child of the King, whose right it is to inherit the throne. You possess princely authority to speak his will into existence on earth!

This royal aspect of our call, as well as giving us access to enormous privileges, also imposes upon us the task of promulgating God's law, and of striving to increase his empire. We dare not restrict our inheritance to ourselves, but must ever seek to bring others into the Father's family.

PROPHETS

> *"You are a royal priesthood ... a people chosen by God to be his own, and called to proclaim the marvellous*

---

[7] 1 Pe 2:9; Re 1:6; 5:10; 20:6; and cp. Is 61:6

[8] These are the ranks, in ascending nobility, of the British peerage.

works of him who brought you out of darkness and into
his radiant light" (1 Pe 2:9).

Note that the terms used by the apostle are collective. That is, he is not speaking so much about the role of each single Christian, but about the character and duty of the entire church. We are a "people chosen by God".

So our royal priesthood is not an individualistic thing; rather, it is a product of our association with the church; it is more corporate than it is private. True, I may, and do, exercise it privately, as part of my relationship with God through Christ, and as the basis of my access to the Father's throne. But I can do so only as I am consciously and certainly a part of the entire "kingdom of priests". Here is a powerful truth; it separates the gospel from all other religions: Christianity does not *have* a priesthood; it *is* a priesthood.

And the church is the vehicle through which that priesthood flows to every believer. If I separate myself from the church, then I am no longer part of that "*people*" called and chosen by God, and I no longer have access to its privileges.

In the NT the terms priest (hierus), king (basileus), and saint (hagios), when they are used in the singular are applied to Christ alone. When applied to the church, they always occur in the plural. This confirms again that we possess priesthood, kingship, sainthood, only while we are in communion with the church (through participation in a local church). There are no separated saints. People who detach themselves from the church detach themselves also from Christ. Mark in the history of Israel that all priesthood was connected, not just with God, but also with the community.

No priest could function outside the borders of Israel. Kingship, too, was meaningless if it was divorced from its social context. Who can be a king in a desert, sans people, sans territory, sans residence? An isolated saint is a living contradiction. We express our sainthood, not by incarcerating ourselves in some hidden cell (like the hermits of old), but through fellowship. Even more, true sainthood is finally realised only in sacrifice for others.

If I am part of the church, if I share its holy destiny, then I take upon myself also the mantle of prophet, which means (said Peter) that I share in the responsibility of "*proclaiming the marvellous works of God*". By my style of life, by word and example, by demeanour and discipline, I should be a living revelation of the power of the gospel to bring a man or woman out of darkness and into the radiant light of salvation.

PRIESTS

> *"You are living stones, who are being built up into a spiritual temple, where you are serving as a holy priesthood. Your offerings are spiritual sacrifices that are acceptable to God through Jesus Christ." (1 Pe 2:5)*

What are these *"spiritual sacrifices"*? They require you to offer to God your

- self Mk 12:32-33; Ro 12:1; 1 Co 6:20; Ep 5:2; Ph 2:17
- sympathy Mt 9:13; 12:7
- substance He 13:16; Ph 4:18

but perhaps highest of all, to offer him your

- song -

> *"The sacrifice that honours (God) most is your offering of praise." (Ps 50:23)*

The first task of a priest is to stand in the presence of the Lord with thanksgiving -

OUR HIGHEST OFFICE

Text: Ho 14:2, 4-7; He 13:15

Hosea says that we should offer God *"the bulls of our lips"* (that is the literal meaning of the Hebrew text). What does that extraordinary phrase mean? It seems to be a colourful way of expressing the same idea as that in He 13:15, *"Offer up a sacrifice of praise to God."* So Hosea was saying, "There is no value in offering God animal sacrifices (bulls, goats, lambs, and so on) unless you are also bringing him a sacrificial offering of true praise. *Other gifts to God should not be neglected; but the gift he desires most of all is the offering of your lips!"* Which raises the question: when is praise a priestly sacrifice?

WHEN IT IS OFFERED IN EVERY SITUATION

Notice that I said "*in*" every situation, not "*for*" every situation, because the latter teaching has been a pestilence in the church. It is inhuman, if not impossible, truly to praise God "*for*" every situation, for there are times to weep, as well as to rejoice (Ec 3:4,5; Ja 5:13; etc.) Indeed, to praise God "for" everything would imply that he is the cause of everything, including sin, crime, violence, divorce, and the like. What an obscene notion!

Thus we cannot praise *God* for things that *Satan* has authored, nor for things that were conceived in the corrupted heart of man and wickedly done against God's very will. But "in" every situation the eye of faith can always see some gift of grace, some miracle of comfort, or of healing. Thus the Psalmist did not rejoice that he was in the valley of the shadow of death, but he could rejoice because he knew even there that the Good Shepherd was still with him (Psalm 23; cp. also Je 31:13).

Now it is not difficult to praise God in some situations - especially those that are pleasant to us. But to set oneself to praise God in *every* situation, that is an act of faith, that is a "sacrifice of praise", and that is the quality of praise God is seeking from us.

That kind of praise is a pure expression of our priestly function.

WHEN IT IS OFFERED IN THE FACE OF DEFEAT

The most difficult time in which to set yourself to praise God is the time of your own defeat. Here are some examples

- when you have had a great miracle of healing but then, some months later, the disease returns with greater ferocity than before

- when, against your expectation, you are dismissed from your job when some cherished goal eludes you

- when, against your own loathing of it, sin has overwhelmed you

- when you have trusted a promise of God and, despite your best efforts to believe, to stand in faith, the promise seems to have failed; and so on.

So, when personal defeat is involved, that is indeed the time when unbroken praise becomes a deep spiritual sacrifice.

What shape should your praise take when it is offered in the face of defeat? What kind of praise would be appropriate, say, if you have just been stricken with a disease that you thought was healed, or overcome by a sin that you thought was defeated? What words should you carry before God on those occasions; what should you say to him?

You would certainly not praise God *because* the problem has returned; but you might praise him for the opportunity to experience a miracle of answered prayer the unchanged reality of the victory that is yours in Christ his unwavering love, which you know will not fail you in your time of need the knowledge that you are still indwelt by Christ, the hope of all glory; for the certainty that you can rise up in the power of the Holy Spirit and crush your enemy underfoot the assurance that your defeat or failure on earth does not affect the righteousness and authority that remains yours in the heavenlies, in Christ and the like.

WHEN IT IS OFFERED IN HONOUR OF GOD ALONE

We do this when we set ourselves to praise God just because he is God, recognising that no other human response to God is appropriate. Whether good things or bad things are happening to you; whether you do or don't feel like praising God; whether he appears to be keeping or denying his promise, you owe God the duty and gratitude of praise.

The Lord deserves our praise as Creator, and because of his holiness, his majesty, his beauty, and his glory. In other words, we should constantly praise God, not just for what he *does*, but rather for what he *is*. But that requires a faith vision, a capacity to see what is invisible; and that is what makes it a sacrifice of praise.

Meditate, for example, on 2 Co 4:16-18. Do you have a vision of that "eternal weight of glory"? Do you know what it means to "look upon the invisible"? Notice how this spiritual perception is an antidote to discouragement and a source of deep inner joy.

But that raises another question: *why* is God so intent upon hearing our praise? Is he just an appalling egotist? Or does he have some higher motive?

Despite the teaching that is popular in some places, God's "ultimate intention" in creating man was not to enhance his own glory, but rather to bring happiness to his children.

Thus he demands that our lips be filled with praise because

- we can be truly happy only when we are serving and worshipping the Lord
- God has decreed that praise alone releases the resources and powers of heaven
- praise is the way to liberty, healing, supply, victory, and so on
- praise is a vital expression of true faith
- praise is a necessary expression of true love
- praise is a sign of real fellowship, of a vital relationship with God.

The early Christians were persecuted, imprisoned, enslaved, not because they preached about Christ, but because they *worshipped* him, and refused to worship any other. That was their chief crime against the Roman state. Even that would have been forgiven if they been willing to offer nothing more than a pinch of incense in a brazier to the "*spirit*" of Caesar. They had but to pronounce Caesar "*lord*" only once, and they might then talk about Jesus as much as they pleased. But they would not do it. Worship, praise, thanksgiving, belonged to Christ alone, and they endured the most awful torments rather than give such priestly reverence to any other being. We too display our royal priesthood never so well as when we stand with uplifted hands and raised voices, proclaiming the splendour and magnificence of our King.

CONCLUSION

"Bring words with you," said Hosea, "and come into the presence of the Lord." He knew the importance of "words". He knew that "words" are an important key to fulfilling our priestly office, especially words of praise. But we need to recognise that praise really becomes praise only when it has a quality of sacrifice about it, when it can be described as "the bulls of our lips"

That kind of praise unveils the image of God in the worshipper; it brings a powerful release of spiritual authority; it strongly moves the Father to act on behalf of the believer; it is the foremost duty of God's royal and spiritual priesthood.

Chapter Three:

CLERICAL PRIESTS

In response to the sneer of the Roman Pope that the Church of England was born out of the lust of King Henry VIII, the urbane and gracious Sir Thomas Browne wrote -

> "It would be an uncharitable point in us to fall upon those popular scurrilities and opprobrious scoffs against the Bishop of Rome, to whom as a temporal prince we owe the duty of good language. I confess that there is cause of passion between us, for by his sentence I stand excommunicated. 'Heretic' is the best language he affords me; yet can no ear witness I ever returned to him the name of Antichrist, Man of Sin, or Whore of Babylon. It is the method of charity to suffer without reaction. Those usual satires and invectives of the Pulpit may perchance produce a good effect upon the vulgar, whose ears are opener to Rhetoric than to Logic, yet do they in no wise confirm the faith of wise believers, who know that a good cause needs not to be patron'd by a passion, but can sustain itself upon a temperate dispute." [9]

In this chapter I must separate myself from the beliefs of some other Christians, and in doing so condemn their less worthy doctrines to the pit. But, like Sir Thomas, I hope to do so without malice or invective; for it may well be that in the reckoning of God some of my own treasured beliefs deserve no better fate. Let Christian charity prevail, though we feel compelled to disagree on certain aspects of doctrine.

---

[9] Op. cit. Part One, Sec. 5.

LAITY AND CLERGY

How foolish are those who deny that God has made room in the church for an ordained, professional, and paid ministry![10]

Paul is emphatic -

> *"God has given some to be apostles, some to be prophets, some to be evangelists, and some to be pastors and teachers. ... Those elders who look after the church, and who do it well, merit double honour. This is especially true of those whose task is preaching and teaching. What does scripture say? 'You must not muzzle an ox while it is treading out the corn;' and, 'The worker deserves his wages'"* (Ep 4:11; 1 Ti 5:17-18).

The pastors and leaders of the church are expected to devote themselves as fully as possible to the work of the gospel, in a manner that would be impracticable for lay people. Special qualities and abilities are required in a "bishop", which other members of the congregation may either lack or not possess to a sufficient degree (1 Ti 3:1-6; etc). The pastors must have time to *"devote themselves to the ministry of the word, and to prayer"* (Ac 6:2-4); they must also be able to set an excellent example of godliness (2 Th 3:7-9; Ph 3:17; 4:9; 1 Co 4:16; 11:1; He 13:7; etc); and they may reasonably expect the people of God to provide them with generous financial support.

But those very factors create a peril in the church. The men and women who are set apart for high office may arrogate to themselves a level of privilege and authority that exceeds what scripture allows. Against all such audacity we press the higher standing of every believing man and woman. In opposition to anyone who claims a special prerogative for some "official" clerical priesthood we insist upon the loftier "spiritual" priesthood of even the humblest saint.

Mark this: *the entire church is a kingdom of priests -*

---

[10] The ideas in this chapter, and the four that follow, owe much to two remarkable books by Dr Cyril Eastwood" The Priesthood of All Believers;" and "The Royal Priesthood of the Faithful;" both published by the Epworth Press, London; the first in 1960, and the second in 1963.

> *"You also, as living stones, are built into a spiritual temple, as a* holy priesthood, *to offer up spiritual sacrifices that are acceptable to God by Jesus Christ ... You are a chosen generation, a* royal priesthood, *a holy nation, a peculiar people, called to sound out the praises of him who brought you out of darkness and into his marvellous light ... (Christ) has made us* kings *and* priests *in the presence of God ... You have made us a* royal priesthood *in the service of God ... Those who share in the first resurrection will be priests of God and of Christ, and they will reign with him for a thousand years.* [11]

Such scriptures declare that from the beginning it has been God's intention to create not just a race, but an *elect* race not just a nation, but *a chosen nation,* not just a laity, but a *priesthood* not just a priesthood, but a *royal priesthood.*

Furthermore, the divine purpose encompasses not just this present time, but the coming age as well; it reaches past the last day to the glorious consummation the Father has planned for his people (Ro 8:19-22). Paul declares that priestly "freedom of access to him "was something that God had long intended to give to his people. It had lain hidden for many generations, but was now accomplished by Christ and revealed in the church. He allows only one qualification: this privilege will lie undiscovered if the people fail to act with the kind of confidence that comes out of trusting the promise of God (Ep 3:9-12).

Now if the royal priesthood embraces the entire church, then every believing Christian must have (as Paul said) unfettered freedom to approach the throne of God. No one can interpose a barrier between us and the Father; no one can claim an *exclusive* right to represent me to God, nor God to me. To all believers belongs the priestly task of mediation; that is, the duty and privilege of representing God to the world and the world to God. If you and I are priests, then we may and must stand before God on behalf of our neighbour, and stand before our neighbour on behalf of God. Always, of course, in the name of Christ, trusting only in the merit that his righteousness gives to us.

---

[11] 1Pe 2:5,9; Re 1:6; 5:10; 20:6.

We cannot, we will not, allow any earthly priesthood to usurp these spiritual rights, nor to preclude us from them. If someone should argue that an earthly priesthood is necessary to stand between God and a fallen society, we reply: "What about the first Christians? Did they need such exclusive mediation?" Of course not. Those early disciples, beginning on the day of Pentecost, were brought at once into an intimate relationship with Christ. They lacked nothing of the grace and power of Christ.

They prayed with force; they were answered with miracles. No ecclesiastical apparatus imposed a barrier between them and the throne. No wall of clerics or bishops had to be surmounted before they could call directly upon the Lord. They knew no priesthood other than that of Christ himself, out of which they discovered their own priestly identity. Further, they came into union with Christ, not by the agency of an organised priesthood (which did not then exist), but in response to the work of the Holy Spirit, and by faith alone.

APOSTOLIC SUCCESSION

How then has the concept risen that lay people have no access to God except through an ordained clergy? Somewhere toward the end of the second century the doctrine of "apostolic succession" developed in the church. An attempt was made to establish an unbroken line of ordination from the apostles to each of the contemporary bishops. The *idea* was that an apostle had conveyed to his immediate successor, by laying-on of hands and prayer, the teaching and ruling authority he had himself received from Christ. Those successors in turn passed on that same apostolic authority to each bishop they ordained - and so on, generation after generation. The *purpose* behind the idea, originally, was to provide stability to the church and to protect it from heresy by insisting that only bishops who stood in the apostolic succession had authority to teach. But the *result* was an arrogation of authority among some bishops (both then and now) that has no countenance in the New Testament.

However, the true "apostolic succession" does not lie in the myth of an unbroken sequence of ordination from the apostles to each succeeding generation of bishops and priests. Rather, it lies in the impartation of grace by the Holy Spirit to each born-again believer, carried back from believer to believer, until we reach across the centuries to the apostles, and ultimately to Jesus himself.

Notice that there are four possible ways to pass on the grace of Christ from generation to generation:

ecclesiastical: that is, by an unbroken line of churches. Yet no denomination or grouping of churches may claim an unsullied descent from the apostolic churches;

episcopal: that is, by an unbroken line of bishops or clergy. But lack of adequate records turns any attempt to trace the modern bishopric back to the apostles into a pious legend;

theological: that is, by an unbroken line of doctrine. The tumultuous quarrels that have rent the church time and again across the years make ludicrous any claim of constancy of dogma. Which leaves one other way:

fiduciary: that is, by an unbroken line of faith. This is the one thing that has remained constant throughout the centuries: simple trust in Christ. The faith that brings his sweet salvation has never changed, nor has the kind of belief in the gospel that rids the soul of death and brings eternal life.

Therefore we say that by the new birth, and altogether sufficiently, each Christian is made a priest and minister before the throne of God. Upon every believer is placed the priestly *privilege* of standing in the presence of God, and the priestly *responsibility* of working, sacrificing, interceding, to bring about a reconciliation between God and mankind.

Although for the sake of good order in the church some are given a special teaching and ruling function, nonetheless the rights and duties of God's royal priesthood belong equally and entirely to every Christian man and woman.

The gospel allows no class of sacrificing priests to interpose itself between ordinary believers and the Father. We dare not depend for our pardon upon the ministration of any priest save that of Christ. We have no need of some other person to intercede on our behalf, for we approach God directly through Christ who himself intercedes for us. We scornfully reject the idea that some ordained person has any greater claim to divine favour than belongs to the humblest believer. Nor can any cleric confer upon me any greater benefit than I am able to seize unilaterally from Christ by unaided faith.

THE LEVITICAL PRIESTS

Another source of the constant tendency in the church to create an official priesthood that stands apart from the laity is the example of ancient Israel. It is true that the priests of Israel, all descended from Aaron, did comprise a separated group with certain functions that were lawful only for them, and other functions that could be more widely shared. In general, the tasks imposed upon the Aaronic or Levitical priesthood were:

- teach the word of God
- care for the sanctuary
- perform the daily rituals
- call the people to worship
- perform the sacrifices
- act as intermediaries before God
- administer the sacred law
- act as the mouthpiece of God.

Those tasks can be divided into two kinds: *ministerial;* and *priestly*. As it was in Israel, so is it still in the church: *ministerial* functions are usually performed by specific individuals who are called and gifted by God, such as pastors, teachers, evangelists, deacons, and the like. But unlike Israel, in the church all *priesthood* is restricted to two entities: Christ (He 6:20; 7:26-27); and the believer (1 Pe 2:9; Re 5:10).

You can search through 1 Corinthians 12:28; Romans 12:1-8; Ephesians 4:11-13, and in places where *bishops* and *deacons* and other *ministry* functions are mentioned, and you will discover an absolute dearth of any word about *priestly* functions. No *sacerdotal* right is conveyed to any *minister* in the church that does not equally belong to every *believer*. In the church there are but two priests: Christ; and the Christian -

THE PRIESTHOOD OF CHRIST

Note that the priesthood of Christ is eternal; that is, his priesthood is inherent in his very nature. He did not become Priest merely as a consequence of the Fall and the need for human redemption. Even if we had never sinned, John 3:16 would have remained essentially true - God would still have loved us; his Son would still have been "given" to us; Christ would still have been the means of bringing us into the higher purposes of God. The apostle was careful to say that "*Christ did not take upon himself the honour of being appointed a High Priest*"; rather, he had always been so in the reckoning of the Father (He 5:5). In affinity with the "order of Melchizedek", Christ was, is, and always will be "a High Priest forever" (6:20; 7:17,21). God has never changed in his intention to give his people priestly access to his throne through the Person of Christ. Human sin obliged the Father to alter his timetable and his method (Calvary became essential); but Christ has from the beginning been designated High Priest by God. He has always been the *Way*, the *Truth*, and the *Life*. It was the love of God, not the sin of Adam, that brought the Saviour into the world.

I admit that we are here confronting one of those "wingey mysteries in Divinity[12]" that Sir Thomas Browne said had "unhinged the brains of better heads" than his.

The church has long been divided on the question of whether or not the Incarnation of Christ was contingent upon human sin. That is, would Christ have been born on earth even if we had not sinned? Some have argued one way, and some the other.

In favour of those who reckon that Christ would not have come among us in the flesh if the Fall had not occurred are such passages as these -

> "*The Son of Man has come to seek and to save those who are lost*" *(Lu 19:10).*

> "*When the time was just right, God sent his Son to be born of a woman, and under the law, so that he might redeem all who are condemned by the law*" *(Ga 4:4-5).*

> "*Here is the reason why the Son of God came: to destroy the works of the devil*" *(1 Jn 3:8).*

---

[12] The full quote reads thus: "As for those wingey mysteries in Divinity, and airy subtleties in Religion, which have unhinged the brains of better heads, they never stretched the *Pia Mater* of mine." (Ibid. Sec. 9; pg. 69.) The "pia mater" is a vascular membrane, or kind of inner skin, that encloses the brain.

Yet each of those passages, and others like them, describe only the manner in which Christ came after sin had entered the world. The style of the Incarnation and its immediate purpose of redemption were forced upon Christ because of the Fall. Such scriptures say nothing about whether or not the absence of iniquity would have precluded the Incarnation. In favour of the idea that God always intended to unite humanity and deity in and through the Person of Christ are arguments like these -

(a) If the Incarnation was in fact contingent upon human sin, then we might well rejoice because of our sin, rather than bitterly regret it. Did it not lead to a stupendous result? Are we not now more highly favoured under the title Sinner than we would have been if we had kept the title Saint? We should find ourselves laughing with St Ambrose: "O happy fault, which has deserved to have such and so mighty a Redeemer!" But that gives sin a greater value than the sinner; as though my *sin* could draw the Saviour to this earth, but I *myself* could not. Yet someone might protest: "Scripture itself declares that Christ came to save his people, and to 'lead many children to glory'!" (He 2:10). True; and it was their *sin* that made the cross necessary; yet even without sin, his purpose to carry them to glory would surely have remained unchanged.

(b) The Incarnation itself is an event of such transcendent wonder, of such miracle and mystery, that it seems impossible to allow as its only cause the capricious behaviour of human beings. Is our iniquity then so powerful? Is God's plan so dependent upon human action? Can we truly argue that we are richer because we sinned than we would have been if we had remained unfallen? It seems better to say that the divine plan has remained constant, and that sin did no more than add an element of atonement and the defeat of death.

(c) Could human sin have changed the dynamics of the kingdom of God? That too seems unlikely. If the redeemed *after* the Fall cannot approach the throne of God except through a Mediator, then they could not have done so *before* the Fall. That is, if Christ today is High Priest, then he has always been High Priest, and will be so forever (He 13:8). No one has ever come to the Father except by him. Even in the Garden, Adam and Eve met

God in the Person of the Logos, as it says in the strange expression used in Genesis 3:8 -

"The man and his wife heard the voice of the Lord God walking in the Garden."

They hid from that Sacred Voice, as it advanced upon them in Eden, just as people today still shrink from fully encountering the Word of God. But encounter him we must, else we shall never draw near to the throne nor ever discover all that the Father designs to give us.

THE PRIESTHOOD OF THE BELIEVER

All priesthood in the church derives from Christ, whose own priesthood was perfected through his :

- *Incarnation*: which fully identified him with our humanity

- *Atonement*: which provided total satisfaction for sin

- *Resurrection*: which created victory over corruption and death

- *Ascension*: which carried him back to his Father's presence

- *Enthronement*: which began his intercessory role in heaven.

Now the Saviour's perfected priesthood is communicated by the Holy Spirit to all who by faith have become part of Christ through his body on earth, the church. This priesthood is available only to a true believer. No one outside of Christ has any access to this royal privilege. Where salvation is uncertain, priesthood remains unknown. That is why so many people in so many churches lack confidence in their approach to God in prayer. Being unsure of their relationship with God, they have no sense of priestly vocation, and no assurance of any right of access to God.

Thus the foundation of our royal priesthood is our justification by faith alone, apart from any merit of our own; for nothing else can bring the necessary stability of soul, security of position, certainty of welcome, and expectation of grace. This justification, this salvation, requires three things:

That God Should Act on Our Behalf

Unless God speaks, there is nothing for us to believe. Unless God acts, faith hangs in a vacuum. All the trust in the world is worthless if there is no divine work in which we can place our trust. Where can hope find a resting place if there is no divine word or deed to fasten upon? Where can love find requitement if the face and form of the Lord remain forever hidden?

Happily, God has acted, and that magnificently, in Christ. At the Cross the work was consummated that despoiled the kingdom of darkness (Cl 2:15), reconciled us to God, created a pathway of victorious life, and opened the way to heaven for all who call upon the name of Jesus.

That We should Respond in Faith

In the great drama of redemption we have this part to play: to believe sufficiently in Christ to be justified from all sin, having abandoned all trust in our own good works. Without such a faith response, God's actions, as far as each unbeliever is concerned, will remain forever unrealised. Unbelief nullifies the promise of God.

That Faith should Act on God's Behalf

Faith that does not act is falsely named. If we have truly believed in Christ, then we will do the works of God - serving him in humility and holiness. But the first and most necessary work is that we should allow our justification to work in us such a boldness of faith that we can brook no hindrance to our claim upon the throne.

Thus we are given the thrilling invitation -

> *"Brothers, God has given us boldness to enter the Most Holy Place by the blood of Jesus. We go in by the new and living way that he has opened up for us through the veil (I mean, his body). Therefore, since we have a great High Priest over the house of God, let us approach God with a sincere heart, holding to an unwavering trust, and keeping our hearts sprinkled and purged of a guilty conscience. ... Let us hold firmly to our confession, and be steadfast in our hope, for the One who gave us the promise is faithful" (He 10:19-23).*

Thus I can say that God has acted *for* me in Christ; and now he acts in me by faith, which itself can only be wrought by his Spirit. The honour must always be all his; no credit accrues to me outside of Christ. Faith is not a good work that scores me points in heaven. Unless the Author of faith implants in me a deposit of trust I am helpless to believe as I should

(Ep 2:8). Yet I must still play my part, which is to arouse that given faith, to employ it to the full for the glory of God, especially by making it the vehicle of a bold approach to the throne.

SALVATION IS THE FOUNDATION

As surely as the priests of Israel alone had access to the inner sanctuary, so we too must become priests before we may boldly enter the Holiest. None, other than priests are permitted to stand in the presence of the Almighty, offering worship and praise, and making intercession. How then can we approach the Lord? We cannot, unless we gain priesthood through entering first into union with Christ by faith. Therefore, where the quality of true faith is lacking, where there is a degree of uncertainty about full justification, there will follow either a denial of the royal priesthood, or a failure to appropriate its benefits. This is the mistake made by certain sacerdotal churches. Because of their perennial uncertainty, or at least ambiguity, about the proposition "the just shall live by faith alone", they are driven both to maintain a separate order of priests and to give them unique powers. In such churches, an ordained clergy is permitted, indeed commanded, to usurp the throne prerogatives that belong to every Christian. To a privileged few are given the heavenly rights that are the property of the entire church.

The importance of good doctrine is now made plain. For when the way of salvation is misunderstood, when the foundation is faultily laid, all else must also be askew. We could sum it up by saying that where there is a mistaken soteriology there will also be a faulty hierology. The correctness of the superstructure depends upon the soundness of the foundation. If a distortion occurs in the doctrine of justification by faith alone, then the concept of priesthood in the church will also become warped. The two are interdependent. When the saints are robbed of their throne rights, then the shepherds will arrogate those rights to themselves. But the end result is actually the complete loss of true priesthood to the entire church. Either all the saints are priests, or no-one is.

Among churches that create a separate priesthood the idea sometimes prevails that apart from the intrusion of a priest the worshippers can neither please God nor commune with him. Yet surely scripture declares that Christ is the one great High Priest who fully imparts to every believer the prerogatives of his own holy priesthood, so that we all, in him, have unfettered access to the throne of God. Refuse to accept a lesser status. God has promoted you; allow neither angel nor man to demote you. Stand firm in your absolute birthright in Christ. If you are part of his royal priesthood then no one can lawfully block your way into the holiest, nor prevent you from enjoying the closest communion with God.

Chapter Four:

BELIEF AND PRACTICE

Perhaps the first man to attempt a restoration of the idea of the royal priesthood, after it had lain dormant for centuries, was Marsiglio of Padua (c. 1275 - 1342). In 1324 he wrote a dramatic work, *Defensor Pacis* ("Defender of the Peace"), in which, among other things, he stressed the rights of the individual Christian over those of the church hierarchy. He argued that the tower of popes, cardinals, archbishops, and so on, was man-made and lacked divine authority. Once his authorship of the book was discovered he had to flee for his life; but he managed to survive and continued to promulgate his ideas. Two hundred years later, his book was still in print, and became a source of teaching for the Protestant Reformers. Indeed, Marsiglio is often described as an unwitting forerunner of the Reformation, which began when Martin Luther first raised a banner against the pretensions of the Roman priesthood. A few years later, in 1523, he sent to the council of the city of Prague some instructions on how to establish a gospel ministry[13]. In his letter he called attention to a basic truth which he reckoned the Church of Rome had perverted

> "A priest, particularly in the New Testament, must be born, not made. He is not ordained; he is created. However, he is not born of the flesh, but of the Spirit, that is, of the water and the Spirit in the washing of regeneration. Therefore all Christians are priests, and all priests are Christians; and accursed be the statement that a priest is something different from a Christian. For this is said without the word of God; it is based on man's word, or on ancient usage, or on the opinion of many who believe it."

---

[13] *What Luther Says*, compiled by Ewald M. Plass; Concordia Publishing House, St Louis, 1959; Vol. III, pg. 1139

Then, in a sermon preached in 1534, Luther thundered: "Every baptised Christian is a priest already, not by appointment or ordination from the pope or any other man, but because Christ himself has begotten him as a priest and has given birth to him in baptism. It is necessary to know this especially because of the papal abomination. The pope has usurped the term 'priest' for his anointed and tonsured hordes. By this means they have separated themselves from the ordinary Christians and have called themselves uniquely the 'clergy of God'[14].

I feel no compulsion to speak as heatedly as Luther did, although the circumstances in which he preached probably required fiery oratory. But the basic idea is valid enough: we cannot allow any body of clergy, no matter how high-ranked they may be, to rob us of the privilege of priesthood.

Luther's doctrine had its germ in the earlier work of Marsiglio. But were the Paduan's teachings truly so radical? Not really, for here is a strange fact: all branches of the church have held, in one form or another, to the doctrine of the priesthood of the believer. The problem is that few have truly practised it. Why not?

Probably because, among other things, it is a frighteningly democratic and levelling truth. If every believer is a priest, and a royal priest to boot, then ultimately every believer holds the highest possible position in the church! That sits ill with those who enjoy supremacy, or who crave hierarchy.

Sadly, both great branches of the church, Roman and Protestant, have often stripped the doctrine of its life -

Rome

(and those who are akin to her in concept) nullifies the scripture in two ways: *First*, (as Luther complained) by restricting in practice many of the functions of the royal priesthood to an ordained clergy; and *second*, by effectively locating the church not in the laity, nor even

---

[14] Ibid. # 3642.

the presbytery, but in the episcopacy - that is, in the company of its bishops.

The idea that the bishops comprise the church is an ancient one. It holds that where there is a bishop there is the church; but where there is no bishop, there is no church

> Cyprian, Bishop of Carthage and a martyr in the third century, held that there was only one Church, that the episcopate founded upon the rock by Christ was in the Church and the Church in the bishop, and that if any were not with the bishop he was not in the Church. Moreover, Cyprian insisted that he who was not in the church was not a Christian, and that outside the church, authenticated by the presence of the episcopate, there was no salvation. [15]

Now there is a degree of truth in that. If salvation depends upon coming into union with Christ by faith, and if Christ as *head* is in heaven, but his *body* the church is on earth, then there is finally no way to relate to Christ except through the church. Can you wed a person's head without also wedding his or her body? Neither can you enter into a union with Christ except by coming also into union with his church. So those who would be sure of salvation must also find a place in the church. But how shall we define the church? Shall we say with Cyprian that the church is the bishop and the bishop is the church? Hardly! I would rather hear the apostle -

> *"You have come to Mount Zion, to the heavenly Jerusalem, to the City of the Living God, and to myriads of angels in festal array. You have come to the Church of the Firstborn, whose names are written in heaven. You have come to God, the Judge of Everyone, and to the spirits of righteous people who have been made perfect, and to Jesus the Mediator of the new covenant, and to the sprinkled blood that speaks better things than the blood of Abel" (He 12:22-24).*

---

[15] K. S. Latourette, A History of Christianity Vol One; Harper & Row, New York, 1975; pg. 132, 133.

Who can doubt that the church consists of the entire company of the redeemed, and that pastors and bishops, deacons and overseers, are but a part of that multitude? So we reject the pernicious narrowing of the church down to a few of its servants, with its inescapable corollary of robbing the people of their priestly heritage. All who are in the church are part of God's royal priesthood; and the church comprises all who have come into union with Christ by faith.

Protestants

In general they hold firmly to the doctrine of the priestly rights of all believers, but they too in practice largely nullify it. They do this in several ways:

- some, by creating a professional priesthood similar to that of Rome, which retains for itself the highest levels of spiritual privilege;

- others, by restricting the people to a low level of expression in worship, which turns them from active participants into passive watchers of a performance by the clergy;

- others, by allowing the people to lapse into a spiritual lethargy that is content never to meet with nor hear from God, nor ever stir itself to reach new heights in faith;

- others, by shredding the scriptures and stripping them of everything supernatural, thus voiding the possibility of answered prayer;

- and others, by reducing the sacraments to mere ceremonies, which prevents them from becoming powerful expressions of the priesthood of the people.

It is surely time for all who believe in the priesthood of the believer to stop giving lip service to the doctrine and to begin observing it in life and in worship. If this were done, then Christian worship would no longer be diminished to a parody presented by the elite. The people of God would no longer suffer themselves to be turned into mere spectators. The pastors of the church would scorn the notion that they have a status before God higher than that of the congregation. On the contrary, shepherd and flock together would acknowledge that they all have full rights of access to God, and of worship, prayer, praise, and intercession.

DOGMA OR DEED?

Merely to hold to the priesthood of the believer as a piece of dogma is futile. It must find a practical outworking in every part of the private and corporate lives of the people. Where this is not done, barrenness must overwhelm the people of God. As an old English proverb says:

"Bad priests bring the devil into church."

The proverb, of course, speaks about a corrupted clergy; but the principle is the same when it is applied to believer-priests.

If God's royal priesthood fails to hold and use its exalted freedoms, then Satan may indeed play a merry game with the saints. The church, indeed the world, would be transformed if every Christian understood and practised his or her royal priesthood! They speak falsely who say that "priests are no more necessary to religion than politicians are to patriotism."[16] .

Without a priesthood there can be *no* religion, for only by the exercise of priestly rights can we safely approach the footstool of the Holy One. However, the priesthood we need is not that of an official class, but the true and universal one made available to the church through Christ. The claiming and exercising of that priesthood by the church would unleash an irresistible surge of spiritual energy across the planet!

Does that seem exaggerated? Then consider the graphic demonstration of this doctrine provided by the explosive growth of early Islam.

Muhammad caught the dazzling idea of the equality of the faithful when the church had forgotten it, and the forces of Islam swept the world. The Prophet built his religion upon three strong foundations:[17] one God; one Book; one Priesthood. The God of Islam is Allah; the Book is the Qur'an; the Priesthood is made up of all Believers. Thus there is no

---

[16] J. H. Holmes (1879-1964) in The Sensible Man's View of Religion

[17] This is a simplified analysis. Muslims themselves would say that their faith stands upon the "Five Pillars of Wisdom": the profession of faith; regular worship of Allah (which includes prayer five times a day); generous alms-giving; the pilgrimage to Mecca; and fasting (especially during the holy month of Ramadan). Some would add to those holy warfare (the Jihad), and the reciting of the Qur'an.

official priesthood in Islam[18]. Each mosque has an appointed leader; scholars who are skilled in Islamic law are highly honoured; These leaders and scholars are given different names, such as imam, mullah, ayatollah, mufti, and the like. but none of those authorities are accorded specific priestly functions. Quite the contrary, any attempt by them to usurp such privileges would be sternly resisted.

As a consequence, in the 7th and 8th centuries Islam exploded out of the Arabian desert. Each warrior was an ambassador for the faith; they were each equal to the other; all were equally bound to the service of Allah; all held the same religious status; and each was expected to be an evangelist for the new faith. Islam surged across North Africa, swamped Egypt and Syria, crossed the sea to what is now Spain, engulfed Persia, and hammered on the doors of the Eastern Roman Empire. Many lands that were formerly wholly Christian overnight became just as wholly Muslim. The church was dispossessed of what had been until then its most populous and prosperous territories. By the early 8th century Arab believers were standing on the shores of the Atlantic in the west, and on the banks of the Indus River in the east.

A stunned Christianity found itself within the space of a generation outnumbered by Islam; only the truncated Eastern Roman Empire remained in Christian hands, along with the barbaric remnants of the collapsed Empire in Western Europe. It seemed for a time that Islam would conquer the world, the Church would be annihilated, and the Mediterranean would become a Muslim lake. That dire fate was averted by a series of notable naval and military victories that the western Christian states finally gained over the Muslim forces[19].

---

[18] J. A. Williams says: "While there is no priesthood or clergy in Islam, there is a class which has played a clerical role in Islamic society, and which has acquired social and religious prestige identical in kind to that enjoyed by the priests of other religions. This is the `ulama' (learned) and the `fuqaha' (lawyers), (who are) the scholars and custodians of the Law. It is they who have traditionally decided what is an `official position'." (The Great Religions of Modern Man: Islam; George Braziller, New York, 1962; pg. 94.)

[19] The story is told in more detail in my book, "The World's Greatest Story," which deals with the first 1,000 years of Christian history.

But the question still remains: what gave such dynamism to Islam? Among several factors that helped the Prophet and his followers to achieve such extraordinary and rapid success is the one we are considering here: the exalted status given to each believer as an equal priest before God.

Yet here is an anomaly. Islam lacks an adequate theological basis upon which to rest its concept of universal priesthood. A satisfactory doctrinal underpinning for this seminal idea can be found only in the church, for it rests our priesthood upon that of Christ. However, in the 8th century (and since), Christians were no longer living out the principles of the royal priesthood. So the church, despite its strong theology, was despoiled by the mosque. Muslims who lacked a sound basis upon which to establish a universal priesthood nonetheless practised it, and were easily able to crush the decadent church.

What might happen today if the whole of Christendom were to awaken again to the realities of the royal priesthood, and begin to practise them in daily life? As Douglas Adams whimsically expressed, nothing is impossible for a people obsessed by a great idea.

Three men - Ford Prefect (a galactic traveller), Arthur Dent (the last human), and a wealthy space explorer Slartibartfast - are conversing together. The explorer wants the two younger men to join him in a mission to save the universe from total destruction by a group of maniacal robots -

> "No," said Ford firmly, "we must go to the party in order to drink a lot and dance with girls."
>
> "But haven't you understood everything I ..."
>
> "Yes," said Ford, with sudden and unexpected fierceness, "I've understood it all perfectly well. That's why I want to have as many drinks and dance with as many girls as possible while there are still any left. If everything you've show us is true ... "
>
> "True? Of course it's true."
>
> " ... then we don't stand a whelk's chance in a supernova ... The point is," Ford said, "that people like you and me, Slartibartfast, and Arthur - particularly and especially Arthur - are just dilettantes, eccentrics, layabouts ...

We're not obsessed by anything, you see," insisted Ford.
... And that's the deciding factor. We can't win against
obsession.

They care, we don't. They win

The world will be won by the people most obsessed with the concepts inherent in the idea of the royal priesthood.

A PRIEST'S WORK

Why is this doctrine so important?

The priesthood of believers arises out of the priesthood of Christ, and is communicated to us along with the new birth.

Therefore since Christ himself, the heavenly High Priest, is the Rock upon whom we are built (Cl 3:11), the exercise of our priesthood in him becomes foundational to vigorous Christian life.

Indeed, all Christian life may be defined as an expression of priesthood, so that where this is not grasped Christian experience becomes dull and prayer ineffective. Mark how each of the major dimensions of Christian life fall within the priestly role: like the priests of Israel we too offer "spiritual sacrifices" of prayer, praise, intercession, blessing, service, charity, rebuke, exhortation, discipline, teaching, proclamation.

Thus we repeat all the work of the ancient priests except that which is Christ's alone: atoning sacrifice; heavenly intercession. In place of that work we simply present Christ himself to God and to the people, just as the ancient priests presented their sacrifices at the altar in the presence of God and of the great congregation.

However, there is a peril in using the ancient priesthood as an example of the spiritual role of the church. Among the Jews the priests became a privileged, moneyed, and powerful group, moving far away from the original purpose of God. A better model is found in the nation as a whole; for just as all Christians are designated royal priests in the New Testament, so in Israel all the people held a mystical priesthood. Israel was called a "nation of priests" -

> *"You shall be for me a kingdom of priests, and a holy nation" (Ex 19:6).*

"You shall be named the Priests of the Lord, and people will call you the Ministers of our God" (Is 61:6).

"From my people will come my priests, says the Lord" (Is 66:21).

As a nation and kingdom of priests, Israel was called to do two prime things: (1) stand as mediators between God and the world; (2) establish its priestly identity by suffering. Those are two of the major themes of the prophets whose oracles show (1) the prophet standing between heaven and earth, interceding for the nation, and declaring the word of the Lord; and (2) portraying Israel in the guise of a Suffering Servant. Four major passages (among several others) take up the latter idea -

"Behold my Servant, whom I uphold; he is the Chosen One in whom I take delight ... He will not cry out, nor lift up his voice, nor call aloud in the street. He will not crush a bruised reed nor quench the smouldering flax until he has established justice and truth" (Is 42:1-3).

"Listen to me you islands, and pay attention all you far off peoples. Long ago the Lord called me, before I was even born, when I was yet in my mother's womb he called me by name.. . And he said to me, `You are my servant, O Israel, in whom I will be glorified.' Then I said, `I have laboured in vain; I have exhausted my strength for nothing; my efforts are wasted.' Yet surely my judgment is in the hand of the Lord, and my work is in his care... And now, says the Lord who formed me in the womb to be his Servant ... I have appointed you to be a light to the Gentiles, that you may carry my salvation to the ends of the earth (Is 49:1-6).

"The Lord God has given me the tongue of one who is learned, so that I may know how to speak a word in season to anyone who is weary ... The Lord God pierced my ear, but I was not rebellious, nor did I turn away from him. I gave my back to the flogger, and my beard to those who tore it out. I did not hide my face from shame; I let them spit on me. I know that the Lord God will help me; therefore I will never collapse in despair. Because I

have set my face like a flint I know that I shall never be ashamed" (Is 50:4-7).

"Behold, my Servant will act wisely; therefore he will be extolled by all and raised to the highest honour and acclaim. Yet just as there was a time, my people, when those who saw you were disgusted, so now they shrink from him. His face was so marred it became unrecognisable; his body so mangled he lost human likeness ... He was despised and scorned by everyone, afflicted with sorrows, and burdened by disease ... But surely he bore our sicknesses and carried away our pains: yet we thought he was being punished by God, broken by sorrow, stricken with disease. But he was wounded for our transgressions, bruised for our iniquities, flogged to bring us peace, and by his stripes we were healed. Like sheep, we had all wandered far away, straying wherever we pleased, but the Lord laid upon him the iniquity of us all. He was bullied, he was beaten, yet he did not complain. Like a lamb in the slaughter house, like a sheep silent in the hands of a shearer, so he kept his tongue quiet. He was taken from prison and deprived of justice; yet who will bother to notice how he was cut off from the land of the living? But for the transgression of my people he was stricken and made his grave with the wicked, lying among the rich in his death. Though he had done no violence, though he had never been deceitful, still it pleased the Lord to crush him and to make him sick... But by his hand the purpose of the Lord will be accomplished. He will see the fruit of his awful labour and be satisfied; by his wisdom my Righteous Servant will bring justice to many" (Is 52:13 - 53:11).

The rabbis rightly applied those oracles to Israel, just as we with equal propriety apply them to Christ. But whether the nation is in view, or the Messiah representing the nation, the principle remains unchanged: the true Servant of God expresses the priestly vocation through suffering. Out of the sacrifice of the Servant for the people comes their salvation. Indeed, the atoning death of Christ was itself born out of and built upon the suffering of the nation, even of those who murdered him. By the same rule, if we are truly members of the royal priesthood then we also have a vocation of suffering -

> *"We have this privilege: not only are we called to believe in Christ, but also to suffer for him" (Ph 1:29).*

Here then are two things that cannot be separated: *priesthood* and *suffering*. Those who embrace the first must be willing for the other; those who shun sacrifice will lose the first. That is, they will lose the benefit of their priestly call. Here as in all things our mentor is Jesus, who did not come to please himself, but rather to make himself servant of all and to ransom with his own life those who turn to God (Mk 10:45). He made himself the *"grain of wheat that falls into the ground and dies"*, and flourishes again in a rich harvest. But if it fails to die, then the field will remain barren (Jn 12:24). Therefore he warned: *if we love ourselves we will be lost; but if we deny ourselves in this world, then life will be safely in our hands for ever* (vs. 25). Those who would follow Christ must also serve him (vs. 26).

What is the foundation of our royal priesthood? Nothing less than the Cross. The Saviour's death and resurrection are the premise of our throne rights. See how indivisibly these ideas are linked -

> *"Jesus Christ is the faithful witness, the firstborn from the dead, monarch over all the nations of the world. He has loved us, and loosed us from our sins by his blood, and he has made us into a royal priesthood so that we might serve God ... You are worth... because you were slain, and by your blood you have purchased people for God from every nation...and you have made them a **royal priesthood** before God, and they will reign over the earth" (Re 1:5-6; 5:9-10)*

Notice the sequence:

- Christ must suffer before he can reign
- now as Sovereign, he creates a kingdom of priests
- that kingdom exists only by the blood, therefore
- those priests are themselves called to suffer and serve
- only then will they gain the throne with Christ.

So then, just as our priesthood arises out of the sacrifice made by Christ, so it must continue to be expressed through suffering by people who are willing to die for the sake of righteousness. This is at least in part the explanation for Paul's strange saying -

> *"What joy it is to suffer for you, so that I may complete by my own body what is still lacking in the sufferings of Christ! I do this for the sake of his body, the church, which God has commanded me to serve" (Cl 1:24-25).*

He surely does not mean that there was any inadequacy in the Cross; rather he is saying that the suffering begun at Calvary did not end there, but must continue to be offered for the world by all who follow in the steps of Christ. It is the chiefest honour given to the royal priesthood, that they are privileged by their sacrifice to have a part with Christ in reconciling the world to God.

Chapter Five:

BISHOPS AND BAKERS

The common Greek verb associated with the work of a special, separate class of priests is *leitourgeo* (from which comes the English word *liturgy*). Here are some random examples from many that occur in the Greek version of the OT -

> *"The bells around the fringe of Aaron's robe must be audible when he goes into the sanctuary to minister before the Lord" (Ex 28:35).*

> *"Whenever Aaron and his sons go into the tabernacle ... to minister ... they shall wash their hands and feet with water" (Ex 30:20-21).*

> *" ... the holy garments of Aaron the priest, and the garments in which he and his sons will do service" (Ex 35:19)*

> *"The Lord separated the tribe of Levi, to bear the ark of the covenant of the Lord, to stand near before the Lord, and to minister and bless in his name to this day" (De 10:8).*

Plainly, *leitourgeo* is attached to the idea of a group of professional priests, standing apart from the people, and possessing certain rights of access to God that the laity do not possess. It is the usual word to describe the office and function of a priest.

But instead of *leitourgeo* (which you would expect to find), the apostles preferred to use *diakoneo*. In fact, *leitourgeo* and its cognates occur in the NT only 15 times, and among them only 6 times in connection with Christian ministers, and not at all in the sense of a special ministering class:

- some teachers, prophets, and others ministered before the Lord in prayer (Ac 13:1-2)

- the Christians offered *service* to each other (Ro 15:27; 2 Co 9:12; Ph:17,25,30)

- the word is applied to the priests of Israel (Lu 1:23; He 9:21; 10:11;)and

- to the angels (He 1:7,14); and

- the Roman civil authorities (Ro 13:6)

- it is applied to Christ (He 8:2,6).

Only once does Paul apply *leitourgos*[20] to himself in anything like the sacerdotal meaning of the word -

> *"God has given me the grace to be a minister of Christ Jesus ... with the priestly duty of proclaiming the gospel of God in such a way that the Gentiles might be offered up to him as an acceptable sacrifice, sanctified by the "Holy Spirit" (Ro 15:16).*

Even that more sacerdotal use of *leitourgos* lacks any exclusive marks; for the "priestly task" Paul accepted is one that is mandated for the entire church: to go into all the world, preach the gospel, and make disciples in every nation (Mt 28:19-20). So in the second century, Irenaeus insisted that "all the righteous possess sacerdotal rank, and all the messengers of the Lord are priests who ... continually serve God and the altar.[21]"

By contrast, *diakoneo* and its cognates occur at least 50 times in connection with the work of ministry that is done in the church both by its leaders and its people. The reader is left with an inescapable impression that the writers of the NT preferred the ordinary word (diakoneo) to the more specialised one (leitourgos), because they wanted to avoid the mistake of establishing an exclusive and privileged class of ministers. The NT insists that the priesthood given to the church does not consist of a certain small group of professionals, but belongs instead by right to every believer.

The testimony of the scriptures listed above, and of the entire NT, is that all the saints are *priests* before God, all are *pastors* of each other, all are *proclaimers* of the mysteries of the gospel, all have *access* to the throne,

---

[20] The noun form of the word.

[21] Against Heresies IV.8.3. "Ante-Nicene Fathers" Vol. One; Eerdmans Publishing Co, Grand Rapids; 1979 reprint of a 19th century work; pg. 471.

all are called to the task of *intercession*, and upon all comes the honour of sharing in the *suffering* of Christ.

These rights and titles cannot justifiably be taken away from the people and restricted to a few ordained clergy. There is no higher calling, no more noble office, no loftier status, no more vital function in the church than that possessed by every believer-priest. All other ministries, every other calling, are only specialised derivatives of this highest estate. Those other forms of service are of course vital to the well-being of the church (as we shall see); but they cannot be allowed to diminish the splendour of the position God has given every one of us in Christ.

AN HONOUR UPON ALL

If what we are saying is true, then the gospel has placed a divine value upon every calling, trade, ministry, profession, or office, from pastor to prince, from bishop to baker, from trustee to tradesman. No distinction is made between them at the throne of God nor in obligation before God. All are obliged to serve the Lord with all their heart; all are deemed to be engaged in full-time Christian ministry; all are expected, by their life, and in their words and deeds, to display his grace and holiness.

Secular workers (so-called) must not separate their church from their job, for they must stand for righteousness in both places. No one can hope to be more godly in church than they are in the outside world. Pious pretence brings no pleasure to the Father; he loathes hypocrisy. Those who understand their role as priests, and who have embraced with joy this sacred office, will never suppose that they may follow one ethic in the house of God and another in daily life. They will not endure a double standard, a variable morality, a piety that is a mere Sunday facade. But where the royal priesthood of the believer has been denied or forgotten (which leads to one standard being adopted for the clergy and another for the people), it is common to find church-going people following different rules on Sunday and Monday.

By contrast, people who have a high opinion of themselves in Christ, and who live in the presence of the Almighty, know that they possess a divine vocation, which they are never free to revoke.

No genuine priest will ever forget that priesthood involves responsibility as well as privilege. Part of that responsibility is to confront and challenge sin wherever one finds it - in the church, at home, at work. Another part is to offer a way of pardon and restoration to the sinner.

Another is to bear reproach for the sake of righteousness. Another is to declare the sanctity of whatever trade, profession, or calling that Christians choose to follow for the benefit of society and the glory of God.

What then is the distinction between laity and clergy? Is there *any* distinction? Are those terms even valid? Should we follow those who deny that there is any place in the church for an ordained ministry. How shall we answer the question -

ARE THERE NO BISHOPS?

Despite the bad press he has received, Korah had the right idea. He and his colleagues said to Moses and Aaron -

> *"You grasp too much for yourselves. Everybody in the congregation is holy, and the Lord is among them. So why do you set yourselves above the people of the Lord? (Nu 16:3)*

No one quarrelled with his affirmation of the equality before God of every man and woman of Israel. But Korah was mistaken when he made that equality the basis of an attack upon the leadership of Moses and Aaron. Those two men had been appointed by God himself for their task. Israel may have been a kingdom of priests; but it still needed leadership. The civil and sacred life of the nation required certain people to occupy positions of high responsibility and authority, which the remaining citizens were obliged to respect. Rule comes from God. Therefore the apostle tells Christian people that they must submit to authority, not just out of fear of retribution, but rather for the sake of a good conscience before God (Ro 13:1-5).

Nothing has changed. As it was then, so today both in the church and in the world, there are necessary rulers whose functions are approved by the Lord. The concept of the royal priesthood does not negate the place occupied in the church by its ordained ministry and other officers. Again the example of Israel is clear. Though priesthood in its deeper, spiritual sense belonged to all the people (Ex 19:5), still the males from the tribe of Levi were appointed to occupy the priestly *office* in the land. Sadly, they abused their privilege, and the denunciation soon became as true of them as it has been of other official priests over the centuries -"Hell is paved with priest's skulls.[22]"

> "I wish I could have the strength of Hercules to purge the world of all vice and sin, and the pleasure of destroying all those monsters of error and sin (the priests) who make all the people of the world groan so pitiably.[23]"

Thomas Fuller, too, tells this story about a man who found himself lost on a bitterly cold night -

> "Having killed his horse, he crept into the animal's hot bowels for warmth, and wrote this with his blood
>
> *"He that finds and brings me to my tomb The land of Plymstock shall be his doom."*
>
> That night he was frozen to death, and being first found by the monks of Tavistock, they with all possible speed hasted to intern him in their own abbey. His own parishioners of Plymstock, hearing thereof, stood at the ford of the river to take his body from them. But they must rise early, yea not sleep at all, who overreach monks in matter of profit! ... (So) the abbot of Tavistock got that rich manor into his possession.[24]"

The Levitical priests gained the same sorry reputation, but could have avoided it simply by remembering three things:

- they were but one of the twelve tribes of Israel and had no *solitary* claim upon divine favour

- the Levite males were set apart as *substitutes* for the firstborn males of the other tribes, whose lives would otherwise have been required of them (Nu 3:5-13; 8:23-26)

---

[22] St John Chrysostom (345-407), "On the Priesthood".

[23] Le Cure', Meslier (1664?-1733); Testament I.2.

[24] The Worthies of England, first published in 1662; The Folio Society, London, 1987; pg. 118, 119.

- they were *supported* by the tithes of the people (Nu 18:21-24).

They were not *solitary*, but one among many; they were *substitutes* not superiors; they were *supported*, not independent. A decent recollection of those facts would have kept the Levites humble, squashing their arrogance, and fitting them to be good servants of God and the people.

Unhappily, there is a constant trend in the church toward corruption. The sequence suggested by Dryden has often occurred –

"In pious times, ere priestcraft did begin[25]"

First God's holy priest*hood*; then an unholy priest*craft*! Yet the antidote cannot be to rid the church of all its ministers, for that too would contradict the will of God. Rather, the people should grasp their own true rights, refusing to yield them to a usurped authority, then their pastors will be kept faithful to Christ. They will be godly shepherds, behaving as servants of the flock rather than tyrants over them (1 Pe 5:1-3).

NO UNIQUE FUNCTIONS?

For many people another problem will arise here. What about baptisms? What about celebrating the eucharist? Surely there are some actions in the church that only a priest/pastor can perform?

We should firmly resist such claims. If all believers are full participants in the priesthood of Christ, then no priestly function exists that is the sole prerogative of a particular group or order of ministers. Some people in the church must be given the duty of devoting their entire lives to the ministry of the word and the sacraments, to prayer, the care of souls, the management of the church, and the like. But they possess no priesthood that differs from or is any higher than the rights possessed by every child of God. Not even their special tasks can be reserved exclusively for them. Whatever they do in fulfilment of their office can and may, if occasion requires, be done by any lay person. We deny categorically that any aspect of Christian ministry or service loses validity unless it is performed by a member of the ordained clergy.

---

[25] The opening line of John Dryden's (1631-1700) poem, "Absalom and Achitophel."

Some might say that we are in violation of John Heywood's 15th century proverb, "Would ye both eat your cake and have your cake?" That is, we want ministers, but would strip them of power. Not at all. There is no conflict between these two concepts: that of the royal priesthood; and that of an ordained ministry. The ministry is set within the universal priesthood of the believers, and must arise out of it, for it is only a particular expression of some of the tasks of that priesthood.

We could approach it another way. The various offices and callings in the church are but specific modes of the divine vocation that belongs to every Christian. Every activity or employment in which Christians are engaged, whether in the church, at home, or in the world, should be viewed as a God-given task. Everything should be done in the name of the Lord, to please him, and for his glory (Cl 3:17,23; Ro 14:7,8; Ep 6:7,8). All are in full-time service for Christ, whether or not they draw their income from the church.

In the world of sport every team must have a captain whose task is to hold the players together and to help each of them play at their highest level of skill. An able captain will give coherence to his team, and membership in the team enables each player to achieve what otherwise would have been impossible. Yet there is no game if they do not all play - neither captain nor players can dispense with the other. All must work together, each recognising the other's specific role.

There we have an illustration of how the church is structured. One of the major purposes for establishing an ordained ministry must be to facilitate the functioning of the royal priesthood. A good pastor will awaken in each member, not a sense of some ecclesiastical privilege and authority that belongs only to the clergy, but rather a sense of their own privilege and authority in Christ –

> *"We are not monarchs over your faith; rather we work with you so that your joy may abound and your faith be always unshaken. ... That is why our preaching is not about ourselves, for we are but your servants for Jesus' sake. Instead we always present to you Jesus Christ as Lord" (2 Co 1:24; 4:5).*

So we are confronted by a paradox. Because no ministry or task in the church can be absolutely restricted to certain persons (for every sharer in the royal priesthood may perform them), therefore some would dispense with the clergy altogether. Yet the NT describes many different offices and clearly establishes a line of command in each local congregation. The reasons are obvious: to establish good order; to maintain discipline; to equip the saints; to create unity; to provide channels through which gifted people may serve the Lord effectively; and the like (Ep 4:11-13).

Luther expressed it like this -

> "Although we are all priests, this does not mean that all of us can preach, teach, and rule. Certain ones of the multitude must be selected and separated for such an office. And he who has such an office is not a priest because of his office, but a servant of all the others, who are priests. When he is no longer able to preach and serve, or if he no longer wants to do so, he once more becomes a part of the common multitude of Christians. ... Some may be selected from the congregation, who then are its officers and ministers, and are appointed to preach in the congregation and to administer the sacraments. But we are all priests before God if we are Christians. For since we are built upon this Stone, who is our High Priest before God, we also have all that he has.[26]"

WHO APPOINTS WHO?

Many questions arise at this point: who appoints the pastors and leaders of the church; how should they be ordained; by what criteria can they be recognised; by whom, how, when, why?

This book is not the place to examine those matters - which are properly the theme of ecclesiology - but let me offer a few ideas.

The mode of calling, ordaining, and installing pastors is not explained in the scriptures. Therefore some would argue that each church is free to adopt whatever process it thinks best; the only restraint being that no clear scriptural principle may be violated. At any rate, if what I have written so far is true, there is no biblical warrant for setting up some mythical "apostolic succession" and then limiting to its exclusive use

---

[26] Op. Cit. # 3644, 3651.

certain roles and tasks. Nor is there biblical authority for placing an absolute barrier around any ministry function in the church. The NT seems to allow freedom to a company of Christians to appoint to the ministry of their local church anyone who gives sufficient proof of a call of God and of conformity to the biblical standards (1 Ti 3:1-12; Ti 1:5-9). The early church apparently took for granted the divine approval of such appointments.

If that freedom does exist in scripture, then there is nothing to prevent a group of churches from joining together and agreeing on certain standards and procedures that they will follow in the training and installing of bishops, pastors, elders, deacons, and so on. Again, the main restraint is that whatever practice they adopt must conform to scripture, and in particular must not impinge upon the rights of God's royal priesthood.

There are at least three parties involved in the task of finding, training, ordaining, and inducting church leaders:

(1) *God*: who must call the minister and equip him or her with the requisite spiritual and natural abilities

(2) *the minister*: who must recognise the divine call, accept it, and prepare himself or herself as well as possible for the task (2 Ti 2:15); and

(3) *the congregation*: which must endorse and appoint the minister, and without whose consent no one can successfully take office.[27].

Upon that basic foundation many other practices may be happily built. But if the foundation itself is disturbed, then harm must fall upon the church.

---

[27] The great Puritan divine, John Owen, wrote in "The True Nature of a Gospel Church", Ch. 16: "Whoever therefore, takes upon himself the pastoral office, without a lawful outward call (that is by a church), doth take unto himself power and authority without any divine warranty, which is a foundation of all disorder and confusion." (Cited by Eastwood.) The idea that ordination for ministry must arise from a local church is true enough, although Owen has perhaps stated it too strongly - yet even he acknowledged that extraordinary circumstances could justify a violation of his rule. However, ordination should be seen as a function, not of some hierarchical figure, but primarily as a function of the local church.

There are two general ways, then, in which the saints can exercise their priestly rights in the local church:

First: by recognising those who are called by God, and by yielding to them the tasks of teaching, disciplining, guiding, and nurturing the congregation.

The nature of those tasks normally requires well-trained and God-gifted men and women who are able to devote their whole time to Christian ministry. When those people are properly appointed, then the congregation will understand that they are representatives, not of some lofty birthright of their own, but rather of the priestly authority of every believer.

Second: by exercising their privilege of unfettered prayer and intercession at the throne of God, offering the godly sacrifices of continual praise, petition, and thanksgiving (He 13:15).

Out of the foundation of the royal priesthood a chosen group of spiritual leaders arises, whose major task is to instruct and perfect that priesthood. Not by arrogating it to themselves, but by expanding it to every saint. Notice the balance that is created:

- Recognition by the *church* of its God-given leadership chains those who would use the priesthood of the believer as a licence to arrogate to themselves any office or ministry they please. They cannot seize a task for which God has not equipped them, and to which he has not called them. Scripture speaks often, and with abhorrence, of those who try to run when God has not commissioned them (Je 14:14-15; 23:21; 29:9; etc.)

- On the other side, recognition by the *leaders* of the priesthood of every believer humbles those who would use their office as a means of personal aggrandisement. It also restrains them from raising barriers across which those who are not ordained dare not pass.

Too often people have felt the exasperation Ophelia expressed, when her brother Laertes exhorted her to maintain her chaste modesty against the blandishments of Prince Hamlet -

> "I shall the effect of this good lesson keep
>
> As watchman to my heart. But, good my brother,

Do not, as some ungracious pastors do,

Show me the steep and thorny way to heaven,

Whiles, like a puff'd and reckless libertine,

Himself the primrose path of dalliance treads

And recks not his own rede.[28]"

The Lord of the church requires shepherd and sheep alike to live holy, upright, and godly lives in this world, while together they wait for the blessed hope, the glorious appearance of our great God and Saviour Jesus Christ.

---

[28] Shakespeare, **Hamlet** I.iii.48-54.

Chapter Six:

BEHAVING LIKE PRIESTS

"Whatever the priest tells you to do, do it; what you see him do, do not.[29] "

The proverb, of course, is a slur upon the official clergy, which has often enough deserved worse. But it is just as appropriate to each believer-priest. We are called not simply to *be*, but also to *do* - that is, to live out in practice what we hold to in doctrine. To be *called* priest is no honour if we do not behave priestly. This suggests that the priesthood must be -

INAUGURATED

UNIVERSALLY

By his death and resurrection Christ perfected himself as High Priest forever and provided the basis for a universal priesthood to be established in his church. That priesthood is co-extensive with the church, will continue until the time of his return, and reach its consummation when the saints stand glorified before the throne.

INDIVIDUALLY

The royal priesthood was installed in the church on the day the church was born; but for each individual it begins at the moment of salvation. This silent and (for many, unknown) gift is an inescapable accompaniment of the new birth. All who are justified by faith are at once brought into the royal priesthood.

---

[29] Greek proverb.

APPROPRIATED

BY FAITH

What Christ has bestowed upon us by gift must be stirred up by faith. The priesthood we have received will no more exercise itself than will any other priesthood.

A millionaire must remain a pauper if he lacks any knowledge of his wealth or how to get access to it. Let us then who are of the royal priesthood learn what Christ has wrought in us; let us seize it by faith, bravely approach the throne, and exercise without fear all our royal prerogatives. Never let the reprimand "Timorous" be deservedly spoken over us. Rather let our glad anthem be -

> No condemnation now I dread,
>
> Jesus, and all in him, is mine;
>
> Alive in him, my living Head,
>
> And clothed in righteousness divine,
>
> Bold I approach the' eternal Throne
>
> And claim the crown, through Christ my own!

BY THE SACRAMENTS

Each of the sacraments of the church is connected with the expression of the royal priesthood in the church, but especially the *eucharist*. There pre-eminently, at the Lord's Table, the believer is brought into communion with Christ, made aware of his or her own in-sufficiency and of the Saviour's all-sufficiency, and brought to rely utterly upon his righteous merits. There in the contemplation of the priestly work of Christ the believer-priest is inspired to godly emulation of the Master. There the saint is emboldened to receive the double kindness of God: the joy of believing in Christ; and of suffering for him (Ph 1:29). There sin is purged and the soul emboldened to go forth and serve the Lord in his own invincible strength. Indeed, I cannot see how anyone who fails to participate in the eucharist regularly can hope to maintain full spiritual vigour.

> In thy truth thou dost direct me
>
> By thy Spirit through the word;

And thy grace my need is meeting,

As I trust in thee my Lord.
All thy fulness thou art pouring -

In thy love and power - in me,

Without measure, full and boundless,

As I yield myself to thee[30].

PROMULGATED

This is the role of the ordained ministry in the church: by precept and example to inculcate among the saints the concepts and practice of the royal priesthood. This cannot be done unless those who are made leaders of the church are people whom God has truly chosen and anointed. No one can *communicate* the dynamics of the royal priesthood unless he or she has first become a *communicant* of it. There is no *impartation* without first an *imputation*. If God has not first given it to me, then I cannot give it to you.

That is why ordination must be an act of God first, and of the church second. The ministering people Christ places in his church are drawn out of the royal priesthood and have the task of bringing the church to a robust expression of its priestly rights and duties.

We might go further and say that unless the ministering people Christ has given to the church are recognised and honoured[31] by it, then the church, and the royal priesthood itself, will collapse and be no more. Apostles, prophets, evangelists, teachers, pastors, bishops, elders, overseers, are all an expression of the royal priesthood in the church; and more, they are an *integral* and *necessary* part of it. Without them the royal priesthood would be unknown; through them it is demonstrated; by them it is encouraged; under them it flourishes; and in them it is powerful.

Another proverb that is scornful of clerics says -

---

[30] From a Communion Hymn, author unknown.

[31] See Ep 4:11-12; He 13:7,17; and the many other scriptures that exhort Christians to honour, respect, obey, and pray for those who rule over them in Christ.

"Priests, friars, nuns, and chickens never have enough." [32]

Rapacity and priesthood have often been linked, to the disgrace of the church. But there is a deeper sense in which the saying is true: genuine priests are never satisfied. Always those who are part of God's royal priesthood want to see it more forcefully outworked: those who are pastors and leaders yearn to equip the saints for service; those who are lay people yearn to see their ministers more powerful in God. Each expression of priesthood arises out of and is dependent upon the other. Where this quality of reciprocity exists, the church will be healthy indeed.

DISSEMINATED

We come now to the main thrust of this chapter: the obligation that lies upon us to *live* the requirements of our priesthood each day. Can you doubt that this high honour impinges upon every facet of Christian life, from its commencement to its climax? Mark, for instance, how at the very beginning of our salvation, our justification by faith locks us inextricably into the character of priests:

- we are justified by faith alone, apart from any work of ours, as an act of the Father's grace, who imparts to us his own infinite righteousness;

- this grace brings us into full union with Christ, and hence communicates to us, by a kind of spiritual osmosis, his own royal priesthood (for if we are one with him, how can we help but share his identity?);

- then, because we are now God's priests, we do what priests do: offer a sacrifice - indeed, two sacrifices: one to reach heaven; the other to reach earth;

- that is, *first*, we turn toward the heavenly throne with an offering of glad worship and grateful praise; and *second*, we take our good works and offer them, not to God (who has no need of them), but to our neighbour (who does need them);

---

[32] An old Italian proverb.

- thus we fulfil the double mandate of a priest: to *face God* in adoration; *and* to *face man* in service.

From then our whole Christian life should be an outworking of priestly action until our earthly pilgrimage is done. Thus the royal priesthood reaches back to our beginnings, carries us through the present, and reaches on into the future. Indeed, if there *were* no future the entire enterprise would be futile beyond measure. Instead it is marvellously reasonable, for all priestly service stands upon the sure hope of resurrection from the dead and of a magnificent inheritance to come.

But let us come back to the present, and look more closely at some of the consequences of this doctrine for the believer and for the church -

ALL SHOULD KNOW

One of the major tasks of the teachers of the church is to make every member of the congregation aware of his or her identity as a member of the royal priesthood. But the same task is also encumbent upon each believer. We all have a responsibility to absorb this knowledge, and then to share it with our fellow Christians. Awareness of the church as a kingdom of priests should permeate the whole body, until all live daily in the strength and delight of this heavenly grace.

ALL SHOULD ACCEPT

If we are all priests before God, then we must all accept the privilege and duty of intercessory prayer, for it is by such prayer that we help to bring about the reconciliation of the world to God. Surely this is a major function of any priest: to stand before God on behalf of the people, pleading on their behalf. Christ himself is our example, who makes intercession for us forever in the heavenlies. By intercessory prayer we truly blend ourselves with Christ and become part of his world-wide redemptive purpose.

Tennyson tells the story of how the dying King Arthur, as he was being carried away in a barge to the mystic isle of Avalon, replied to the tears of the last of the knights of the Round Table, Sir Bedivere -

> And slowly answer'd Arthur from the barge:
>
> "The old order changeth, yielding place to new,
>
> And God fulfils himself in many ways,

Lest one good custom should corrupt the world ...

If thou shouldst never see my face again,

Pray for my soul. More things are wrought by prayer

Than this world dreams of. Wherefore let thy voice

Rise like a fountain for me day and night.

For what are men better than sheep or goats

That nourish a blind life within the brain,

If knowing God, they lift not hands of prayer

Both for themselves and those that call them friend?"[33]

ALL SHOULD UNDERSTAND

We cannot be content merely to know that we are a royal priesthood; we need also to grasp what this *means* - that is, to know our rights in Christ, the freedom we have to draw near to God, our spiritual authority over all the powers of darkness, our claim upon the Father's bounty, and the like. Yet even that is not enough. Knowing that you are a priest and knowing your priestly rights may still prove futile unless you have a heart to rise up and claim those rights.

David recognised this principle - although it seems to have been only a single flash of illumination, for he never again referred to it. He began *Psalm 4* with the abrupt words: "*Answer me when I call upon you, O God of my right!*" In Hebrew, the statement is almost rude. It is a sharp demand, a bold imperative. Indeed, it reads so pungently that few translators can bring themselves to render it literally, so they employ various softeners, such as "*God of my righteousness*", or "*my righteous God*". But David was made of braver stuff.[34] He demanded that God should uphold his rights and give him all that lay in the divine promise.

---

[33] Alfred, Lord Tennyson, "Morte D'Arthur." Emphasis mine.

[34] At least, he was brave for the moment. The Hebrew phrase he used in Psalm 4:1 occurs only here in the entire OT. It seems that neither David, nor anyone else, was ever bold enough to use it again!

Many Christians refuse to think of themselves as having *any* rights. Quite the contrary; in an excess of self-abnegation they protest that they have no rights at all, that they are worms deserving nothing good from God, and that any blessing the Lord deigns to give them comes solely from his merciful grace. Of course, that is partly true; but it ignores what God has clearly done for us in Christ and the rights by which, through that same grace, he has ennobled us. So let us not cravenly follow those timorous souls who shrink from the seemingly scandalous claims of scripture. Rather, let us gallantly seize what belongs to us in the gospel, audaciously demand that God must honour his word. We should expect him to respect our rights, heed our cry, and make our priesthood effective for his glory!

ALL SHOULD COMMUNE

From the divine viewpoint, the chief joy that arises out of the royal priesthood is the basis it provides for unbroken fellowship between God and his children. Only because Christ has imparted to us his priesthood do we have a right of access to the throne. Without a priestly identity we could never lawfully enter the Holy Place. Instead, we would be like those ordinary Israelites who faced instant death if they tried to enter any part of the temple where only priests were allowed. But we *are* priests; therefore we have full rights of entrance, and one of the most certain marks of our priesthood should be a state of constant communion with the Father. By day, by night, at work or play, in church or out of it, our hearts should be in a state of continual worship, praise, thanksgiving, prayer, and simple delight in the presence of the Lord. If many Christians are far removed from that happy condition, it is because they have failed to appreciate or to use their freedom as members of the royal priesthood.

ALL SHOULD SHARE

One of the great words of the church is *koinonia*[35] It means *"fellowship"* - but not just in the sense of friendship. *Koinonia* has no true equivalent in English, for the Greek word carries a deeper sense. It describes

---

[35] "Koinonia" and its cognates can be found in Ac 2:42; Ro 15:26; 1Co 1:9; 10:16,18; 2 Co 1:7; 8:4,23; 9:13; 13:14; Ga 2:9; Ep 3:9; Ph 1:5; 2:1; 3:10; 1 Ti 6:18; Phm 1:6,17; He 10:33; 13:16; 1 Pe 5:1; 2 Pe 1:4; 1 Jn 1:3,6-7; plus other places.

friendship that is expressed through caring, loving, and sharing. No one could claim *koinonia* who ate while his friend was hungry, or who laughed while his friend wept, or who had little interest in sharing his friend's triumphs and defeats. *Koinonia* implied a desire to associate with each other as much as possible, to participate in each other's happiness, to help carry each other's burden - it was at least as much a thing of sympathetic *action* as it was of mere words or sentiment. Parsimony could never journey comfortably with *koinonia*, for those who owned this fellowship delighted to share their possessions and joys with each other. This was a friendship marked by liberality and companionship. Christians who had discovered koinonia saw themselves as partners in pilgrimage; they had no wish to travel alone, but sociably reached out in warm love to their fellow pilgrims. They were comrades in arms; allies in battle; workers in righteousness; equals in freedom; participants together in the same grace of God; co-inheritors of the same splendid glory.

Yet this quality of divine koinonia is often lacking from the church, which instead is frequently rent by envies, hierarchies, cruelties, and other sad signs of a people governed more by an instinct to grab than to give. Why? Because when the concept of the royal priesthood is abandoned, then the basis for maintaining an equality among the people will be lost. But if they all see each other as possessors of identical priestly rights before the throne of God, then none can be exalted above the other, nor can one deserve higher honour than the other. All the members of the royal priesthood will be eager to esteem each highly in Christ, and to strive for the sweetest unity among them. To be otherwise is to offend the Lord –

> Sacrifices there were among the Jews; sacrifices there are, too, in the church: but the species alone has been changed, inasmuch as the offering is now made, not by slaves, but by freemen. ... (But) God is not appeased by sacrifice (alone). For if anyone shall endeavour to offer a sacrifice merely to outward appearance, unexceptionably, in due order, and according to appointment, *while in his soul he does not assign to his neighbour that fellowship with him which is right and proper*, nor is under the fear of God; - he who thus cherishes secret sin does not deceive God by that sacrifice which is offered correctly as to outward appearance; nor will such an

oblation profit him anything ... Inasmuch then as the church offers with single-mindedness, her gift is justly reckoned a pure sacrifice with God."[36]

ALL SHOULD SERVE

Since every believer is an equal member of the royal priesthood, then all have an equal duty to serve the King and the interests of the kingdom. None are excused from this service. All should be active in ministry. There is a task in the church and in the world for every Christian to fulfil. Nor is one role greater than another in the reckoning of God. Success in this kingdom is not measured by statistical *achievement*, but by *faithfulness*. We are all called to find the place God has appointed for us, and to serve him with all our heart. For us there is no distinction between secular and sacred employment; we are all full-time servants of the king. Whether within the church or outside it, every Christian has a divine vocation to fulfil. Nor is position in the kingdom dependent primarily upon human talent, but mostly upon the sovereign choice of God, who may call whom he will into any office or function, whether in the world or in the church.

ALL SHOULD WITNESS

Christ laid upon the entire church the Great Commission: *"Go into all the world, preach the gospel, and make disciples"* None are exempt from that charge. We all have a mission to the world. When Israel was commissioned as a kingdom of priests, this was one of the prime reasons: to bring to all nations the knowledge of God, and to teach them all to worship him as Lord. They were to shine as the light of God in the world, bringing all the peoples of the earth to fear the Lord and to bow before him alone. They failed, because they forgot who they were. The church too has a dismal record of poverty in fulfilling the missionary mandate of Christ. And for the same reason. If all Christians would rise up in the riches of the royal priesthood, full of the Word and the Spirit, going in the name of Jesus, then the radiance of the gospel would swiftly spread to the ends of the earth.

---

[36] Irenaeues, Against Heresies IV.18.3,4. Op. cit. pg. 485.

ALL SHOULD SACRIFICE

Possession of the royal priesthood cannot be separated from that which was central to Christ's priesthood: the cross. So he bids us to deny ourselves daily, take up our cross, and follow him.[37] Nothing less will suffice to mark us as his disciples. Now this means that the true aim of a Christian in this life is not *happiness*, but *suffering*, not *pleasure* but *holiness*. Happiness and pleasure will undoubtedly be large components of our lives; but they cannot be our goal. We are cross-bearers. We are a sacrifice upon the altar of human redemption. We cannot take the place of Christ, but we complement his pain, and show ourselves his followers by sharing in his suffering for others. In the writings of the apostles, the concept of the royal priesthood is always set within a framework of the sacrificial work of Christ. For example -

> *"(Jesus is) the Living Stone, who is precious to God, and chosen by him, although the mob rejected him. You are like him - living stones, whom God is building up into a spiritual temple, in which you are a spiritual priesthood, called to offer spiritual sacrifices that are acceptable to God through Jesus Christ. ... (Jesus is) the Stone that the builders rejected, which has now become the capstone ... And you are a chosen people, a royal priesthood, a holy nation, the people who belong to God ... (therefore) I urge you, since you are pilgrims and strangers in this world ... to live with such excellence among the pagans, that although they charge you with wrongdoing they cannot help but observe your good works, and so glorify God" (1 Pe 2:4-12).*

How shall we suffer for Christ? What are these *"spiritual sacrifices"* we are called upon to offer? Those are difficult questions; but my next chapter attempts an answer.

---

[37] See Mt 10:38; 16:24; Mk 8:34; 10:21; Lu 9:23; 14:27.

Chapter Seven:

LIVING SACRIFICES

In the 5th century before Christ there were two great wars between the Persians and the Greeks. In one of the early campaigns news was brought to the Persian emperor Darius that the city of Sardis had been taken and burnt by the Athenians and Ionians. The ancient historian Herodotus describes what happened then -

> "When Darius learnt of the disaster ... he asked who the Athenians were, and then, on being told, called for his bow. He took it, set an arrow on the string, shot it up into the air and cried: `Grant, O God, that I may punish the Athenians.' Then he commanded one of his servants to repeat to him the words, `Master, remember the Athenians,' three times, whenever he sat down to dinner.[38]"

We Christians would find it useful if someone would do the same for us: every day to repeat three times the injunction, "Remember the Cross!" For the mark of discipleship is not the pursuit of comfort but the act of daily denial, of taking up the cross, and of following Christ. The chief act of a priest is to offer sacrifices on the altar of God. If we are priests, then sacrifice is integral to our identity and to our task. Except that in our case (following the example of our High Priest) the sacrifice is not something external, rather, it is *ourselves* (Ro 12:1). Here then is a mystery: the one sacrifice made by Christ is more than sufficient to redeem the whole world; yet without the sacrifice we too are called to make, the world will not be redeemed. We are to be suffering partners with Christ in bringing the world to reconciliation with God. How shall we do this? By suffering

---

[38] The Histories Book Five: 105; tr. by Aubrey de Selincourt and A. R. Burns; Penguin Books, London, 1972; pg. 382. The Roman orator Cicero called Herodotus "the father of history".

INWARDLY

BY CLAIMING ACCESS TO THE THRONE

Surprisingly, there is an element of spiritual sacrifice involved in the very act of claiming our priestly rights of entrance into the holiest. To make this claim, to express it in prayer, to fulfil it by faith, are all acts of war against our fallen nature. As Paul says, the *"flesh"* is at war with the Spirit, hungering for what the Spirit opposes, and hating what the Spirit desires (Ga 5:17). Therefore it takes a certain ferocity to throw down that carnal nature, and to stand firm in the promise of God. That is why Paul again says that we must "put to death everything that belongs to our fallen nature" by fixing our eye with unyielding determination upon the heavens, where Christ is sitting at the right hand of God (Cl 3:1-5). And Jesus said, even more pungently, that *"the kingdom of heaven suffers violence, as violent people take it by force"* (Mt 11:12).

People who have no heart for such spiritual warfare will abandon the challenge, and their rights will be usurped by the enemy. But those who are ready to strap on their spiritual armour, and by the shield of faith and the sword of the Spirit thrash the enemy - though the battle may be weary and long - will find the measureless reward of God (Ep 6:10-19).

BY MAKING INTERCESSION BEFORE THE THRONE

We show ourselves true priests when we intercede with God on behalf of others, for intercession is proper work for a priest. And it *is* work![39] Some intercession can be fiercely laborious.[40] But this is a true oblation, a spiritual holocaust, that we can offer God. Even the Hebrew prophets foresaw the day when such sacrifices would be chosen by God in place of the animal immolations of Israel. The 3rd century lawyer and Christian apologist Tertullian, wrote about this –

> "The church will achieve excellence when, for the purpose of honouring and extolling God, it strives together to offer him, like a chosen victim, its most

---

[39] Hosea 14:2; Hebrews 13:15.

[40] See Ro 8:26-27; and think about the intensity of Jesus' prayer in the Garden (Lu 22:14).

precious sacrifice of prayer. For this is the spiritual victim by which the primitive animal sacrifices have been abolished. That is why God said to Israel: `What do you mean by all these countless sacrifices? I am gorged with your endless offerings of rams and of the fat of your plump cattle. I never had any liking for the blood of bulls, sheep, and goats. Whoever told you that I wanted you to bring such things with you when you came into my presence?' (Isaiah 1:11).

"What then *does* God require. The gospel shows us the answer: `*An hour will come,*' says he, `*when those who truly adore the Father will worship him in spirit and in truth. For God is a Spirit, and rightly demands that those who love him worship him accordingly.*[41]`

We are his true lovers and his true priests who, by praying in the spirit, (1 Corinthians 14:15; Ephesians 5:19; 6:18; Colossians 3:16; Jude 20.) by offering a sacrifice in spirit, of prayer - a victim that is altogether suitable and acceptable to God. That is the sacrifice he has required; that is the one he has long waited to receive from us. See this victim: devoted without reservation to God; nourished by faith; guarded by the truth; with innocence unsullied; pure in virtue; and garlanded with adoration. When such an offering is accompanied by the splendour of a righteous life, surrounded by psalms and hymns as it approaches God's altar, then it will obtain for us everything God has promised.[42]"

Accordingly, when Paul began to list what his young protege Timothy should teach the church to do, he said -

"First of all, make sure that requests, prayers, intercession, and thanksgiving are made for everyone - especially for all rulers, and for those in high office" (1 Ti 2:1).

---

[41] John 4:23-24.

[42] On Prayer; paraphrased from the "Ante-Nicene Fathers", Vol. III.

There is the *"first"* duty of the royal priesthood, to take upon itself the burden of mediating between God and the world in prayer. An open environment in which to proclaim the gospel, and the degree of community response to it, depends upon how well the church performs this assignment. A church that fulfils its priestly duty of intercession will please God, for its people have become sacred partners with him in the work of salvation (vs. 2-4).

OUTWARDLY

BY SACRIFICIAL SERVICE FOR THE CHURCH

Paul cites the example of the first converts in Asia, the household of Stephanas, who *"devoted themselves to the service of the saints"* (1 Co 16:15). Can someone be truly called *Christian* who has no care for a fellow believer? The people who deserve to be honoured in the church, says Paul, are those who cheerfully supply what others are lacking (1 Co 16:17). How well the scriptures speak about the charming Dorcas, who was always "busy doing good, and helping those in need" (Ac 9:36). Hence she was easily called a *"disciple"*, because she followed in the steps of the Master. Paul was not too proud to describe his ministry as one of "service to the saints"(Ro 15:25); and he warmly commended Phoebe, whom he described as "a servant of the church ... and a wonderful helper of many people" (16:2). We should be like the saints at Macedonia, who despite severe persecution and extreme poverty, were so full of the joy of Christ that they pleaded for an opportunity to help. So too we should count it the highest privilege not to rule others, but to serve them (2 Co 8:1-4). But the Macedonians were not alone; for the Corinthians also were anxious to play their part in serving other Christians, and they set an example that stirred other churches to action! (2 Co 9:1-2). Then there was Philemon, in whom Paul found great joy, because he was a man by whom many of God's people had found refreshment (Phm 7).

Therefore all who revel in the title "priest" will also gladly heed instructions like the following-

> "Share what you have with needy people in the church, and be hospitable to all" *(Ro 12:13)* ... "Open your houses to each other, without complaint; for if you have received a gift from God you should use it in the service

of others. Then you will be faithful stewards of the many different gifts God has planted among you" *(1 Pe 4:10).*

Now the rendering of such generosity, support, openness, and help to other people often comes with pain. People can be ungrateful, they take advantage of you, they may despise you even while they strip you bare.

So this service can truly be a sacrifice. Yet it will bring a rich reward -

> *"Your cheerful service not only meets the need of God's people, it becomes also a source of boundless gratitude to God. ... Those who have received your assistance will loudly praise God when they see that you do not merely talk about your faith in the gospel of Christ, but you back it up with obedient action. They will heartily thank God for the way you have given so generously, both to individuals and to the whole community. Such a demonstration of the riches of grace that God has given you will make them send out their hearts to you in fervent prayer" (2 Co 9:12-14) ...*

> *"You should never suppose that God might unjustly forget all the labour you have done for him, and the love you have shown by eagerly helping his people. ... So don't become lazy now, but keep on imitating those who through faith and patience will receive the inheritance they have been promised" (He 6:10-12).*

BY SACRIFICIAL SERVICE FOR THE WORLD

About 150 years after the resurrection of Christ, Irenaeus, who occupied the dangerous office of bishop of Lyons wrote a treatise against heretics. In it he scorns people who suppose that the gospel has opened the way for them to enjoy every carnal fancy, and to live a life of sensual self-indulgence. He talks about what it means to walk as a disciple of Christ -

> "(Their doctrine) is refuted by the teaching of the Lord, with whom not only is the adulterer rejected, but also the man who desires to commit adultery; and not only is the actual murderer held guilty of having killed another to his own damnation, but the man also who is angry with his brother without cause: who commanded his disciples not only not to hate men, but also to love their enemies;

and enjoined them not only not to swear falsely, but not even to swear at all; and not only not to speak evil of their neighbours, but not even to style any one 'Raca' and 'fool'; declaring that otherwise they were in danger of hell-fire; and not only not to strike, but even, when themselves struck, to present the other cheek to those that maltreated them; and not only not to refuse to give up the property of others, but even if their own were taken away, not to demand it back again from those who took it; and not only not to injure their neighbours, nor do them any evil, but also, when themselves were wickedly dealt with, to be long-suffering, and to show kindness toward those that injured them, and to pray for them, that by means of repentance they might be saved.[43]"

Thus the early church resolved to live by the rule of Christ, and to follow the example of selfless sacrifice that he had set. Not a life of vengeance nor of indulgence, but of gentle sacrifice, marked by a heart to give, and give yet again. The end result, said Irenaeus, was a church powerfully equipped by the Holy Spirit to overcome the kingdom of darkness -

"Wherefore also, those who are in truth his disciples, receiving grace from him, do in his name perform miracles, so as to promote the welfare of other men, according to the gift which each one has received from him. For some do certainly and truly drive out demons, so that those who have thus been cleansed from evil spirits frequently both believe in Christ and join themselves to the church. Others have foreknowledge of things to come: they see visions, and utter prophetic expressions. Others still, heal the sick by laying their hands upon them, and they are made whole. Yea, moreover, as I have said, the dead even have been raised up, and remained among us for many years. And what shall I more say? It is not possible to name the number of gifts which the church, scattered throughout the

---

[43] Against Heresies II.32; op. cit. Vol One, pg. 408.

world, has received from God ... and which she exerts day by day for the benefit of the gentiles ... for as she has received freely from God, freely does she also minister to others." [44]

There seems to be a sad contrast between the way the earnest bishop spoke about the supernatural ministry of the late 2nd century church, and the behaviour of some pentecostals and charismatics in our theme. All too often, the miraculous gifts of the Spirit are today used more to promote the name, fame, and fortune of the minister than they are to serve the world. But see how Irenaeus explains the purpose for which his church sought and employed the charismata: "so as to promote the welfare of other men ... And, according to the gift which each one has received from God, so the church exerts herself day by day for the benefit of the gentiles ... For as she has received freely from God, freely does she also minister to others."

Man-made priesthoods have commonly served their own interests more than ever they have served the people. But when God creates a priesthood, he designs it to benefit the flock more than the shepherd.

TOTALLY

SACRIFICED IN WORSHIP

We are called not merely to *present* a sacrifice, but rather to make *ourselves* a living sacrifice on the altar of God. This, says Paul, is true spiritual worship, and the only way to discover and realise the good, pleasant, and perfect will of God (Ro 12:1-2).

One way we do this is by *"offering to God a continual sacrifice of praise - the harvest of lips that confess his name"* (He 13:15).

When is praise a sacrifice? Simply, when you determine to praise God *"continually"* - whether you feel like it or not; whether heaven is responsive or silent; whether you are triumphant or defeated, prosperous or poor, winning or losing! Worship is not so much an experience to enjoy, as it is a sacrifice to offer; especially by the presentation of ourselves fully to God in praise, and prayer, and the total surrender of

---

[44] Ibid. pg. 409.

our lives to his will. Pre-eminently, this complete devotion of body, soul, and spirit to the glory of God, as a spiritual sacrifice well-pleasing to him, should be expressed through the eucharist.

Thus Justin Martyr wrote in the middle of the second century – "Being vehemently inflamed by the word of his calling, we are *the true* high priestly race of God, as even God himself bears witness, saying that in every place ... sacrifices are presented to him (that are) well-pleasing and true. Now God receives sacrifices from no one, except through his priests. Accordingly, God, anticipating the sacrifices which we offer through this name, and which Jesus Christ enjoined us to offer - that is, in the eucharist, with the bread and the cup - and which are presented by Christians in all places throughout the world, bears witness that they are well-pleasing to him"[45]

SACRIFICED IN SERVICE

There must be in us a willingness, not only to *live* for Christ, but better, to *die* for him - in the service of the gospel and of the world. How else can we claim to be followers of Jesus? How else can we display the priesthood we have received from him? The beauty and glory of the church is displayed most fragrantly when her people become a company of consecrated priests, devoted to worship and witness, intercession and service, for the glory of God alone.

CROWNING GLORY

Notice again that our union with the priesthood of Christ makes each believer an active participant in his three great offices of

PROPHET

My mind is open to receive, and my ear hears, the word of the Lord spoken from heaven. What God gives me, I speak as the oracle of God (1 Pe 4:11, KJV). He may tell me of things past, present, or future; he may speak out of scripture or apart from scripture (though never against

---

[45] Dialogue With Trypho ch. 116,117; op. cit. Vol. One, pg. 257. Emphasis mine.

scripture); and what he gives me I must be willing to utter, and the church must be willing to hear (1 Co 14:30-31).

PRIEST

In the exercise of my priestly title I draw near to God with no fear of rejection. No barrier exists between me and the living God. My natural place is at his very footstool. He has already blessed me with every spiritual blessing in the heavenlies, and there I am already enthroned with Christ (Ep 1:3; 2:6). Presenting the blood of Christ is all the plea I need to capture the totality of the Father's favour and to be the recipient of all his grace.

KING

There on the throne with Christ, at the Father's right hand, I share his monarchy over the kingdom of darkness, treading the Serpent underfoot (Ro 16:20; Lu 10:19; Mk 16:15-18). Nothing except my own unbelief can prevent me from completing all that he has given me to do and becoming all that he has called me to become (2 Ti 4:7-8).

Now note that I gain all this immediately from Christ himself; it is not subject to any control by some other priest or church official. I need no intermediary to stand between me and God, nor will I accept one. Should any dare to interpose himself where only Christ should stand, he will be roughly pushed aside! Did any of the apostles ever attribute to themselves some priestly function that was not equally the birthright of every believer? Christ alone has certain priestly functions that must ever be his unique privilege; but everything that remains is the property of the entire church and of every person in it. Let no one rob you of it!

So we can say that this doctrine of the royal priesthood is the crowning glory of the gospel and of the purpose of God. As we began, so shall we end, rejoicing throughout the eternal ages in our priestly identity -

> *"Those who rise in the first resurrection will be priests*
> *of God and of Christ, and they shall reign with him!"*
> *(Re 20:6).*

Chapter Eight:

INTO THE HOLIEST

Text: Hebrews 10:19-25.

The apostle describes the place where we Christians worship, and he gives it two localities: the house of God in heaven; and the church of God on earth. There we find four great gifts from the Lord -

WE ARE GIVEN BOLDNESS

"Therefore friends, we are given great boldness to enter into the holiest by the blood of Jesus, by the new and living way that he has created for us through the veil - that is, his body" (vs 19-20).

Now that the blood of Jesus has been shed, and its power and virtue given to us, we should shake off all timidity and fearlessly come into the closest presence of God. Full liberty is given to every believer to stand in the holy of holies. We have this confident trust in the Lord: if we lay claim to the blood of Jesus and seek an audience with him, he will at once draw us up to the throne. We may not see God. We may not even feel his presence. But, though we have not moved a step, we know that the moment we claim his attention, he will be there with us to hear our prayer.

No one who believes in the blood of Jesus should ever feel any shame about approaching God. The door of the palace opens to anyone who turns the magic key of faith. The day will come when we shall literally enter the holy of holies, and take our seat with Christ at the right hand of God. But why wait until then? All the real benefits of that access are available to us now!

What are some of those privileges? If you step into the holiest in Jesus' name, what will you find? Among other things:

- we may enjoy the cleansing provided by the blood that is sprinkled on the mercy seat;

- we may revel in fellowship with the great God whose glory shines there;

- we may eat of the heavenly manna that is kept there, the bread of life which a man may eat and never die;

- as Aaron's flowering rod was in the ark, so we may find the comfort and guidance which the Shepherd's rod and his staff still give, and his resurrection power;

- as the cherubim overshadowed the mercy seat, so may we claim the protection and help of the mighty angels of God;

- there we can find refuge, forgiveness, healing, the answer to every cry of our hearts.

Make use, then, of this matchless privilege. Be bold to believe that, by the blood of Jesus, you may immediately step up and stand in the protection of the throne - "the secret place of the Most High God". There Satan dares not enter; there is eternal security. In every time of need, in every moment of temptation, you may in faith pull up the four walls of that heavenly sanctuary around you - walls that are firmly established on the solid silver foundation of Jesus' blood. What enemy will there be who can then harm you? In that place, like your Lord, you may confidently wait in expectation of your adversary's inevitable downfall!

In former times, the holy body of Jesus stood between us and the heavenly sanctuary, just as the heavy curtain of old veiled off the inner part of the tabernacle. But Jesus allowed his body to be torn and, in doing so, both closed off the road to the old tabernacle in Jerusalem and initiated a new pathway, which leads straight to the heart of heaven!

The great sanctuary in the heavens has been dedicated to the use of men and women; it is thrown open to all who desire to enter there - always providing they seek to enter with hearts that are sprinkled with the blood of Jesus. The apostle says that

THE WAY INTO HEAVEN IS "NEW"

That is, it is fresh, vital, effective. It will never grow old, will never become outdated, nor be superseded. The first covenant decayed, waxed old, and vanished away. But this will never be said of Christ. The way he has opened is ever new - each time a sinner comes to it, he finds that it speaks to his heart, confirms his need, satisfies his conscience.

Familiarity will never dull its value. Constant use will never wear it out! But also

THE WAY INTO HEAVEN IS "LIVING"

The body of Christ was broken, the veil was rent asunder, but he rose again. He lives for evermore! This is no defunct ritual; it can never die. Though he was once wounded, Christ now lives to make intercession for the saints. This way is "*living*", because the more Christians make use of it, the more strength it gives them. Though they come to it deadened by sin, the moment they set foot on it they are made alive unto God. Though they come to it weary and defeated, the moment they touch it the wings of an eagle will be given them, to carry them into the heavenlies where the Lord himself will nourish them.

The blood of Jesus was shed. The body of Jesus was broken. He was stretched upon the cross. And God has made that cross into a bridge from earth to heaven. By it we may enter boldly into the holiest.

WE ARE GIVEN A HIGH PRIEST

> "*Since we now have a **High Priest** over the house of God, let us draw near with a true heart and in full assurance of faith. Come with your hearts cleansed of an evil conscience, and your bodies washed with pure water (vs 21-22).*

"We now have a *High Priest*". Literally, an exceeding great priest, none so powerful, so noble, so exalted, we had better make sure we do not despise the grace of God by ignoring his provision for us. Rather let us, without fear, obey him, and enter boldly into his presence; for in Christ we are freely granted full access into the holiest and all its privileges.

The "*house of God*" has a High Priest. Individually we are called the "temple of God"; therefore we, each one, have in Christ a personal priest. This has great value, as even the people of long ago recognised. See Judges 17:7-13. Micah knew the value of a priest and, having obtained one, sincerely claimed God's blessing - "Now I know that the Lord will do me good, seeing I have a Levite to be my priest." While he was misguided in his actions, and violated scripture (because he knew no better, cp. vs. 6), yet he was right in principle. Unfortunately, Micah's attempt failed. He was robbed of any blessing he might have gained because, as the next chapter records, another employer offered the priest a higher salary. So he promptly left Micah to serve them!

But we have a Priest who will never violate his agreement with us! He is our own Priest, established in our own house. Having him as our Priest, how much more will the Lord do *us* good!

Christ is the High Priest of all believers: so to him each one may go with perfect freedom (no Israelite ever had such access to Aaron); but also he serves the church collectively. The congregation that knows the High Priesthood of Christ and avails itself of his ministry is a church that will excel in the abundant blessing of God. Its worship will be carried on, as it were, within the very walls of the Holy of Holies.

Before we can draw near to God, certain requirements must be met - though they are all given to us by Christ. Just as Aaron had to clothe himself in sacred garments before entering the Holy Place, so must we receive these from Christ and clothe ourselves with them before we approach the throne -

"A TRUE HEART"

That is, a heart honest in its motive, and sincere in its intentions. There can be no deceit in the soul of a man or woman who approaches God. Their hearts must be faithful to God, genuine in their love for God, not harbouring any rebellion against God.

"FULL ASSURANCE OF FAITH"

Are you planning to go into God's presence? Then you must do so with unshakeable confidence that he will receive you gladly. If you have doubt in your mind, if you lack conviction, if you are not prepared to lean fully upon him, having absolute trust in his goodness - if you fall short in these things, you cannot please God. We must be thoroughly convinced, as we kneel in prayer, that when we call upon the name of Jesus and claim his blood, we will be instantly carried into the holiest.

"CLEANSED OF AN EVIL CONSCIENCE"

An "evil conscience" is one that keeps on accusing you long after it should be silent. Reject that false voice; knowing yourself to be free of all condemnation, because of the merits of Christ and the washing of his blood. Refuse to yield to feelings of guilt. We must have a conscience so cleansed that it knows what is truly good and what is really evil; a conscience that longs for righteousness, yet rests in Christ; a conscience that by no means glosses over sin, but trusts in the blood; a conscience that scorns the lies of Satan, yet remains sensitive to the whisper of the Holy Spirit.

"BODIES WASHED WITH PURE WATER"

The priests of old were obliged to wash before entering the tabernacle; so also must we. This pure water is the *Word of God* and the *Spirit of God* -

> *"Christ sanctifies and cleanses his church by the washing of water by the word" (Ep 5:26)*

> *"We are not saved by any work of righteousness that we have done, but only according to his mercy, by the washing of regeneration and renewal by the Holy Spirit" (Tit 3:5)*

> *"Now you are clean through the word that I have spoken to you" (Jn 15:3).*

WE ARE GIVEN A CONFESSION

> *"Let us hold fast to the confession of our faith without wavering, for the One who promised is faithful" (vs. 23)*

What is that confession? Nothing less than a sure expectation of triumph over every enemy, and the certain confidence that God has heard us and received us. This hope we are expected to seize, steadfastly maintaining our confession of it. In our confession, there should be no uncertainty, no wavering. Having a hope of God's blessing, and a promise of being able to enter the holiest by the blood of Jesus, we must cherish it, nourish it, allow it to burn bright and clear, acknowledging both that God is fully able to deliver us, and certainly will deliver us (see Ja 1:4-8).

The ground upon which the apostle bases his exhortation to hold fast to our confession of faith is the faithfulness of God. In every way, the Lord is reliable, his promise may be fully trusted. Those who trust in God will never be ashamed. It is impossible that God should fail, or that his promise should prove to be a lie.

WE ARE GIVEN A DUTY

"Let us watch over each other, provoking one another to love and to good works. Nor should you forsake the assembling of yourselves together, which some have turned into a habit. Rather, you should exhort each other with growing urgency as you see the Day approaching" (vs. 24-25)

The passage we are considering (He 10:19-25) comprises an exhortation that is a practical application of those three great eternal virtues named elsewhere by Paul: *Faith; Hope; and Love* -

- "Let us draw near in FAITH"
- "Let us hold fast to HOPE"
- "Let us urge constantly to LOVE"

If (as some think)[46] Paul was the author of *Hebrews* then our text (He 10:19-25) was written by the same man who wrote *1 Corinthians 13:13*; so we may have here his own sermon outline based on that text. The passage may then form an interesting comment on the meaning Paul himself ascribed to the words "faith", "hope", and "love":

> **FAITH** is the quality that gives us confident access to God
> **HOPE** is the quality that gives us steadfastness in trial
> **LOVE** is the quality that results in mutual help and good works.

Within this framework we are instructed to

"WATCH OVER EACH OTHER"

The word means *"to observe fully"*, which leads us to a remarkable train of thought. We are to pay careful attention to each other; closely notice

---

[46] The authorship of the Letter to the Hebrews has been questioned from earliest times. For example, in the **City of God** (early 5th century) Augustine wrote: "Many important things are written about Melchizedek in the letter that carries the title `To the Hebrews'. The majority of people attribute this letter to the apostle Paul, but there are others who deny his authorship." (16.22). The "majority" Augustine mentions only applied to the eastern churches. The churches in the west in the main denied it.

each other; look deeply into each other's lives with a view to discovering those things that are good and bad, and determine how the good may be encouraged, and the bad obliterated.

Now diligent practice of such "considering" could lead to untold strife if it were not balanced by this: we are so to consider each other that the result will be to stir up love. If our paying attentive care to any person engenders anger and accusations of "busybodying", we had best change the method of our "considering"! We should so study to take care of our fellow Christians that we cause them, not to resent us, but to have a greater love for us.

So it is our duty to incite each other to greater love for each other, for the church, and for our heavenly hope and righteousness. This "provoking" of each other should stimulate ourselves and our brethren in Christ to a love that is active, a love that produces good works. By example, by word, by manner, we should make it our aim to incite such love in the hearts of all, and thus become the instigators of many helpful deeds. Our behaviour should be such that it encourages others to a more noble life, a life well pleasing to God.

Then we are also exhorted to

BE DILIGENT IN WORSHIP

He said that we must not *"forsake the assembling of ourselves together"*. The expression *"not forsaking"* means particularly *"to desert"*. Because of persecution, many were deserting the church and falling back into their old life. Every such person was a bitter blow to the church and to its witness. A major reason for the *Letter to the Hebrews* was to provide a powerful argument against such desertion. In a time of persecution, possibly the worst fault a Christian can make is to apostasise - that is, cravenly to save life or property by renouncing the church and by turning one's back on Christ.

The apostle may also have been referring to a habit of many of the Greeks of the day. It was customary for a person to go through all the initiatory rites of a particular sect or cult, but then, once initiated, to go no further. Simply to gain admittance to the group was considered the most important thing. Possibly there were many people who had progressed as far as baptism, and had been made members of the church, but then saw no further need of fellowship.

But Christians are called by God into fellowship. While salvation may be an intensely personal matter, Christian **maturity** springs from a proper "family" life with other brothers and sisters in Christ. There is a tendency among some Christians to be "lone wolves" - but that attitude is sternly denounced throughout the whole New Testament. The habit some people have of neglecting attendance at church must be rejected by anyone who truly loves God and is led by his Spirit. So we find that a mark of a true saint is this -

> *"Lord, I love the house where you dwell, and the place where your honour resides"(Ps 26:8).*

> *"This one thing have I wanted from the Lord, and will keep on asking for: just to stay in the house of the Lord every day of my life. I want to behold the beauty of the Lord; I want to worship him in his temple"(Ps 27:4)*

> *"Happy are all those who dwell in your house; they will never stop praising you!" (Ps 84:4)*

> *"Just one day in your courts is better than a thousand anywhere else. I would rather be a doorkeeper in the house of my God, than to live where wickedness pitches its tent" (Ps 84:10)*

> *"I was glad when they said to me, Let us go into the house of the Lord" (Ps 122:1).*

We are required, therefore, to *"assemble ourselves together"* - not just to assemble, but to assemble together: to gather in complete fellowship; to assemble in harmony; to recognise that each believer present is a member of the entire body of Christ, and that if *"one member suffers, all the others suffer with it; if one member rejoices, all the others rejoice with it"*.

Just as a machine is carefully assembled from its constituent parts, so should we gather for worship in such a way that each member coheres with the other -

> *"Behold, how good and how pleasant it is when brethren dwell together in unity! ... That is where the Lord commands his blessing; that is where you will find life for evermore" (Ps 133:1-3).*

Then he said that we must

"EXHORT ONE ANOTHER"

Here again is a vital duty. Wrongly performed, it may lead to great unhappiness. Rightly performed - in a true spirit of love, grace, and humility - it will bring great encouragement to many trembling hearts.

The word translated *"exhort"* has some fascinating shades of meaning. Here are a few of them-

> call each other nearer together
>
> invite men to the salvation of Christ
>
> ask of each other assistance and protection
>
> implore each other to show goodness and mercy
>
> strongly urge each other to steadfastness
>
> give ready consolation to each other in trouble
>
> warn each other of faults
>
> advise each other against wrong doing
>
> instruct each other in righteousness

Those things, and many like them, we are commanded to do, especially at the time of our assembling together.

Then the apostle gives a major reason for the urgency of his demands -

"BECAUSE YOU SEE THE DAY APPROACHING"

To the writer and his readers, that day was particularly the day of the destruction of Jerusalem, which Christ himself had warned them of (Mt 24).

To us, that day is the approaching day of Christ's return. Many will blaspheme the Name of God in the day of wrath that is coming; many will lose their first love, many will fall away. Therefore it is very needful for us never to neglect attendance at the Christian assemblies, and to be careful to exhort one another. Only thus will we be able to stand in that dreadful day, and to have confidence when we are called into the judgment of God.

Chapter Nine:

FALLING INTO PERIL

Here is another anecdote from Herodotus

> "The Spartans were the first to get the news that Xerxes was preparing an expedition against Greece ... The way they received the news was very remarkable: Demaratus, the son of Ariston, who was an exile in Persia (learned) that Xerxes had decided upon the invasion of Greece (and) felt that he must pass on the information to Sparta. As the danger of discovery was great, there was only one way in which he could contrive to get the message through: this was by scraping the wax off a pair of wooden folding tablets, writing on the wood underneath what Xerxes intended to do, and then covering the message over with wax again. In this way the tablets, being apparently blank, would cause no trouble with the guards along the road. When the message reached its destination, no one was able to guess the secret until, as I understand, Cleomenes' daughter Gorgo, who was the wife of Leonidas, divined it, and told the others that, if they scraped the wax off, they would find something written on the wood underneath. This was done; the message was revealed and read, and afterwards passed on to the other Greeks."[47]

As soon as I read that story I realised that it was an apt illustration of our relationship with the scriptures. The Bible is like those wooden tablets. Its best message is in a sense "waxed over". If you don't know how to look for it, you won't find it. That is why people can read the Bible all their lives yet never discover what is really written there. To paraphrase Paul a little: "No eye can see, no ear can hear no mind can grasp what God has prepared for those who love him, unless God reveals it to us by

---

[47] Op. cit. Book Seven: 238; pg. 524.

his Spirit" (1 Co 2:9). Mere literacy and intelligence are not enough; to catch the wealth of scripture there must also be *revelation*, a kind of inner enlightenment. The word of God needs to be illumined by the Holy Spirit so that we can see the glory of God beyond the printed page (Ep 1:17-18). Without such a quickened eye and opened ear, we remain like those ancient Greeks: we hold the message in our hands, but cannot read it! We need the Holy Spirit to scrape off the wax, to unveil our vision, to inform our understanding.

Nowhere is that more true than for the doctrine we are considering: the royal priesthood. This truly is one of the "mysteries" of the faith: a doctrine apparently easy to understand with the mind, yet worthless unless it is perceived in the spirit. That is also true of this aspect of the royal priesthood: the sacrificial task of the priest, and the warning given to those who do not fulfil their calling. Thus we come to our text for this chapter: *Hebrews 10:26-31*. Some have called this the most awesome passage in the whole of the New Testament. There are strong words here. Behind them we sense the passion of the apostle's burning love for righteousness. We see here what Peter meant when he said-"

> *The time has come when judgment must begin. It will start at the house of God; and if it begins with us, what will happen at the end, when it falls upon those who disobey the gospel? If the righteous can hardly be saved (as scripture says), how then will the ungodly and the sinner fare?"(1 Pe 4:17-18).*

I do not want to soften the impact of the harsh words used by the apostle in this solemn passage; but nor do I want to press his warning beyond a reasonable boundary[48]. Let us pray for a true revelation of the Spirit as we look at this

---

[48] I mean Hebrews 10:26-31. This passage notably, but also others like it, have been softened too much by Calvinists, and hardened too much by Arminianists. The first want to remove it from the church and apply it only to those who seem to be Christians but are not. The second want to read it so sternly that all confidence is taken away from the believer. The first are trying to preserve the eternal security of the believer ("once saved, always saved"); the second want to preserve our freedom either to accept or reject Christ at any time.

These five headings are spread through this and the following two chapters.

Remonstrance
Reason
Recompense
Remembrance
Reward.

THE REMONSTRANCE

"If we wilfully persist in sinning after we have learned the truth, there can be no further sacrifice for sins. Nothing is left but a fearful looking forward to judgment - a fiery indignation that will consume in its flames every enemy of God" (He 10:26-27).

"Fearful!" That is the word used by the apostle. Is he talking about Christians or about sinners? I have no doubt (from the terms he uses) that these warnings are addressed to Christians -

"for if we sin"

"after we have learned the truth"

"by which we were sanctified"

"the Lord will judge his people"

"you were enlightened"

"you endured that fierce struggle"

"you shared the suffering of others"

"you joyfully accepted the confiscation of your goods"

"you know that better possessions await you in heaven"

Notice the pronouns *"we"* and *"you"*, which plainly refer to the apostle himself, his companions, and to the Hebrew Christians. Also several of the other expressions can only belong to people who are truly saved, who have been cleansed from their sin in the blood of the Lamb. So it is possible for Christians to *"persist in wilful sin"*, and to lose their grip on Christ. Why? How? Because (he said) *"wilful sin"* means

"treading under foot the Son of God"

"treating the blood of the covenant like a profane thing"

"insulting the Spirit of grace"

Now a person whose sin requires such expressions as those to describe it has done far more than just yield to temptation. This is not sin that results from some sudden attack of Satan, or arises from force of circumstances. Nor is it the sin that stems from yielding to some vile habit, which the soul loathes even while coming under its bondage.

Exactly what kind of sin is referred to in this passage? In the 30th verse, the apostle quotes from the Hebrew scriptures and says, "For we know the One who said, `Revenge is mine, and I will surely take it;' and again, `The Lord will judge his people.'" It follows that the kind of sin he is speaking of echoes the example of Israel in which a clear distinction was made between two kinds of sin: *ignorant*, and *wilful*.

Under the laws of Moses, no atonement or pardon was offered for deliberate or presumptuous sin. The sacrifices covered only what Moses called sins of *"ignorance"* - among which were included sins of impulse and passion, sins that sprang out of the heat or pressure of the moment. In other words, sins that a good man or woman would instantly regret, and of which they would at once repent. For such sins an offering acceptable to God could be made. But there was no provision for deliberate, coldly chosen, pre-meditated, or wilfully stubborn crimes against the divine law.

> *"If someone does something that violates one of the Lord's commandments, but was unaware of committing a fault ... then he must bring a goat as a sin-offering to the Lord" (Le 4:2 ff.) ... "If you inadvertently fail to carry out any of the commands that the Lord has given ... then you must present a goat as a purifying offering, and the priest will make an atonement for you before the Lord, and you will be forgiven" (Nu 15:22-29).*
>
> *"If someone, whether native-born or an alien, sins deliberately against the command of God, then that person has mocked the Lord and must be put to death at once. Anyone who wilfully despises the word of the Lord and breaks his law must be put to death. Guilt of that sort cannot be removed."(Nu 15:30-31) ... "Anyone who contemptuously rejects the ruling of a judge or of a*

ministering priest must be put to death. That is the only way to purge Israel from evil" (De 17:12).

The existence of those laws caused David's despairing lament. His murder of Uriah was a cruelly calculated crime, one that was impossible to explain or excuse. So he knew that none of the ritual sacrifices could offer him any protection. There was no atonement he could make, no offering he could bring. Nothing was left, except to throw himself upon the mercy of God, trusting that the Lord would show him kindness -" In your unfailing love, be gracious to me, O God, and blot out my iniquity according to your limitless mercy! Wash away my uncleanness, and purge away my sin, for I cannot shake off my wickedness and my crime is always before me. Only against you have I sinned, O Lord, doing what was hateful in your sight. ... Create in me a pure heart, O God, and put within me a renewed and faithful spirit. Do not drive me away from your presence; do not remove your Holy Spirit from me; but give me back the joy of your salvation, and help me by giving new strength to my spirit" (Ps 51).

Against that background we can now ask what the apostle means by "*wilful sin*"?

What is sin? We may define it as "any voluntary transgression of the law of God." Sin occurs when a known divine law is violated, or when a positive divine rule or command is voluntarily neglected. The word in the original means literally "to miss the mark", "to offend God", "to trespass against God". Now we may be guilty many times of these things without falling under the severe judgments outlined here. For it is not the simple transgression of the law which is under examination, but such transgression when it is committed *wilfully*.

What does that mean?

The warnings the apostle gives are dreadful in their import. Therefore we need to define carefully and truly the limits of what he means.

The primary sense of "*wilful*" is "*voluntarily*" - that is, without constraint. To act in a voluntary manner is to act without an external influence or force interfering to cause that action. Voluntary sin is a sin that a person commits of his own free will, out of his own determinate choice, without being prompted or compelled into that sin by another. An involuntary action cannot be deemed either good or evil; it is morally neutral.

The Greek word occurs in only two other places in the New Testament - in *Hebrews 10:26*; and in *Philemon*. When he wanted Philemon to be kind to his runaway slave Onesimus, Paul said - "I would have preferred to keep Onesimus with me, so that he might care for me on your behalf while I am here in prison for the sake of the gospel. But I would not do such a thing without first consulting you, for I want your kindness to be a result of your own **free choice**, not forced upon you against your will" (Phm 14).

"Wilful" sin then, is not the sort that results from being mastered by an overpowering desire that one has struggled against in vain. Nor is it sin that a person is driven to by circumstances beyond his control. *"Wilful"* sin is done by deliberate design, with cold intention, knowing that it is sin, and not caring that it is sin. This is sin committed willingly, of set purpose, without any concern for the law of God or for the anger of God. It arises from an obstinate mind, a perverse heart, a stubborn intention to do wrong.

The people to whom the apostle addressed his warning had *"learned the truth"*. They had not merely "heard" the gospel, but had acquired the knowledge of the gospel. They had *"got hold of"* the truth - as the Greek word implies; they had fully recognised the truth of the Gospel; they had once acknowledged that this was the only way of salvation. In the gospel, they had distinctly seen the wrath of God and the mercy of God; they had learned to discriminate between good and evil; they knew what was true and what was false. To know such things and yet to set oneself deliberately against them, without any fear of God or man, is surely to be placed outside the benefit of sacrifice.

So he said, *"there remains no other sacrifice for sins"*. How is this? Simply because, having destroyed faith in Christ by such behaviour, they had banished God's only provision for salvation. If anyone rejects Christ, they must die in their sins, for God will appoint no other sacrifice for sins. But there is encouragement here also. For while the sacrifice of Christ was so entire that God made it the only accepted sacrifice, so that "there remains no *other* sacrifice", it is also certain that the sacrifice of

Christ *does* remain. And it will always be effective for any who turn from their sin in deep repentance and fasten their faith in him.

But, "*how shall we escape if we neglect such a great salvation?*" What other sacrifice can atone for sin? What other offering will God accept? If a man despises Christ, how then shall he be saved? What other prospect has he than to fall under the heavy wrath of God? Nothing is left for him but "a fearful looking forward to judgment".

There is actually a word missing from that translation, the Greek indefinite pronoun *tis*, which means "a certain one ... a kind of ... in a manner" and the like. Thus the clause would be more accurately translated as "a kind of fearful looking forward to judgment"[49] The old KJV had "a certain fearful looking for", which was perhaps misleading. The word "certain" should not be read in its positive sense of something definite and unavoidable, but rather in an indefinite sense. So the translation "kind of" is better.

Now this introduction of an indefinite element into an otherwise very strong statement is important. It suggests that a person who once commits such wilful sin is not *inevitably* doomed to inescapable destruction. The significance is rather that such wilful sin is desperately dangerous, because it has in it a tendency to harden the heart into final rejection of Christ. Only if (or when) such a final rejection occurs will the sinner actually be cut off for ever from the presence of God.

People who are in peril of becoming "wilful sinners" would do well to start "*fearfully looking for*" the day of doom. Contemplation of it might bring them to repentance! The phrase means literally, "*a frightful and terrible prospect*". So it is actually a description of the judgment, not of the attitude of the sinner. Someone who has truly become a "*wilful sinner*" has no fear of the anger of God, no expectancy of judgment. Both words are used only in this epistle: "*looking for*" occurs only here; "fearful" also occurs in 10:31 ("It is a *terrible* thing to fall into the hands of the living God"); and 12:21 ("So *terrible* was the sight, that Moses said, 'I am quaking with fear.'") In all three passages the word is clearly descriptive more of an awful fact than of human fearfulness. Thus the

---

[49] See similar expressions using "tis" in Lu 1:5; 17:12; Ja 1:18; etc.

dread power of sin: it so dulls the conscience that not even such an appalling threat can awaken the wilful heart.

What is this *"frightful and terrible prospect"*? He describes it in three expressions-

"JUDGMENT"

Those who die outside of Christ will be obliged to stand before the judgment of God. They will hear the sentence of doom being pronounced by the irresistible voice of God, a sentence which, once written in the book, may never be revoked. A sentence described as -

"FIERY INDIGNATION"

That is, the white hot fury, the burning wrath, the fierce anger, of an offended Deity. Such despicable, wilful sin against the knowledge of the Son of God can issue in nothing but the extreme ire of God and the utter contempt of the holy angels. Such sin must be strongly abhorred by the church; it merits stern rebuke, and tearful pleas to be reconciled to God - which, of course, is the thrust of *Hebrews*. But if such solemn warnings are ignored, then the end is inevitable -

CONSUMED IN FLAMES

With a breaking heart he warns that the fiery indignation of God *"will consume in its flames every enemy of God."*

Who were these enemies of God?

They were Christians who stopped going to church! And, doing so, they fell into sin, became hardened in that sin, refused the salvation of Christ, crucified fresh the Son of God, and so brought themselves under judgment.

Here then is his remonstrance -

> *"Do not forsake the assembling of yourselves together; for if we sin wilfully, there remains only an awful prospect of judgment."*

This theme is continued in the next chapter.

Chapter Ten:

RHYME AND REASON

"There passeth a story commonly told and believed, that Edmund Spenser presenting his poems to Queen Elizabeth, she, highly affected therewith, commanded the Lord Cecil her treasurer, to give him a hundred pounds; and when the treasurer (a good steward of the queen's money) alleged that sum was too much, 'then give him' (quoth the queen) 'what is reason;' to which the lord consented, but was so busied, belike, about matters of high government, that Spenser received no reward. Whereupon he presented this petition in a small piece of paper to the queen in her progress:

> I was promised on a time,
>
> To have reason for my rhyme;
>
> From that time unto this season,
>
> I received nor rhyme nor reason

"Hereupon the queen gave strict order (not without some check to her treasurer) for the present payment of the hundred pounds she first intended unto him."[50].

That incident is the origin of the phrase, "without rhyme or reason", which might well describe the behaviour of those foolish people who figured at the end of the previous chapter. It also leads on to the second part of our argument, which began with the apostle's *"remonstrance"*, and now continues with

THE REASON

> *"Anyone who scorned the law of Moses was put to death without mercy following the testimony of two or three*

---

[50] Thomas Fuller; op. cit. pg. 262

witnesses. How much more awful do you suppose the punishment should be for someone who has trodden under foot the Son of God? Such people treat as if it were a profane thing the blood of the covenant, by which they were sanctified, and mock even the gracious Spirit himself" (He 10:28-29).

Notice here two things: the severity of the crime against Moses, the *Servant* of God; and the severity of the crime against Jesus, the *Son of God* -

THE SEVERITY OF THE CRIME AGAINST MOSES

... the servant of God

The apostle draws our attention to those who *"despised"* the law of Moses, and to the penalty they suffered. What does it mean, to *"despise"* the law? Faults like the following:

- to reject the warnings of the law, as did the Pharisees who, having no fear of God, *"rejected the counsel of God against themselves"* (Lu 7:30)

- to spurn the teacher of the law, as did the people when they turned aside from Christ, and Jesus rebuked them: "Anyone who *rejects* me, and refuses to heed my words, has one who will judge him" (Jn 12:48)

- to count that law as worthless, as it is said God will do with the vaunted learning of carnal man: "I will *bring to nothing* the wisdom of the intelligent" (1 Co 1:19)

- to make that law void, as Paul was afraid of doing with regard to the gospel: "I do not frustrate the grace of God" (Ga 2:21)

- to throw that law aside, as Paul said some had done with the gospel: *"They deserve damnation because they have thrown away their first faith"* (1 Ti 5:12).

In all those scriptures, the same word is used as in our text. To "scorn the law of Moses" (or to commit the parallel crime of wilful sin against the gospel) means more than just breaking that law, or even disobeying any of its particulars. Rather it means disobedience that is not followed by repentance. To "despise" the law of God is to join deliberately with those who

count it as a contemptible thing,
set it aside,
consider it worthless,
consistently violate it,
openly reject it,
proudly cast it off,
wickedly scorn it.

A person may be caught up for a while in the pleasure of sin without becoming guilty of deliberately placing God's law in contempt. When faced with a divine warning, such a person will tremble in fear, deeply repent and turn back to God.

But the wilful sinner has no such contrite heart. Having a low opinion of scripture, disdaining its warnings, ignoring its pleas, he is without hope of the mercy of God.

Under the law of Moses a person guilty of such calculated sin was condemned to death.

However, the law-breaker could not be executed unless the crime was fully confirmed by at least two or three witnesses. The act had to be witnessed; the prisoner's attitude had to be established - was the sin done in "ignorance" or "presumptuously" (Nu 15:24-31)? The rule was strict: the death sentence should be pronounced only after

> *"you have been told about it, and you have heard the evidence yourself, and after diligent enquiry have found the report is true and thoroughly confirmed ...*

Sentence of death may be executed only upon the evidence of two or three witnesses. The testimony of two or three witnesses shall be enough to warrant putting someone to death; but no one is to be condemned upon the word of only a single witness" (De 17:2-7).

The law of Moses was severe. But it was just.

THE SEVERITY OF THE CRIME AGAINST JESUS

... the Son of God

We may reasonably suppose that, as the blessings of the new covenant are immeasurably superior to the old covenant, so its punishments will also be more severe. Do you imagine that the greater privileges of the gospel bring with them a lesser responsibility than was required under the law?

Think! says the apostle. How could you suppose that God will ignore those who despise his Son? Mark how fierce was his denunciation of a man who only violated the sabbath! (Nu 15:32-36) But which is the greater sin: to scorn the Saviour; or to scorn the Sabbath? The greater the crime, the greater the condemnation. Therefore the face of God is set hard against those who continue in wilful sin; a sterner, heavier punishment must be meted out to them. This must be a penalty far worse than was ever written into the statutes of the old law, for that dealt with the body alone, whereas this will deal with both body and soul.

Yet the sentence of God will strictly conform to the sin. Each will receive only the punishment proper to the sin. None will receive a heavier rod than is deserved; none will receive less. Each will receive such punishment as fits the crime (Lu 12:47-48).

What is this crime?

It has before been spoken of as "*wilful sin*" and "*despising God's law*". Now it is opened for us more particularly –

Punishment will fall upon all who trample God's Son

> "To trample upon an ordinary person shows intolerable
> insolence; to treat a person of honour in that vile manner
> is insufferable; but to deal thus with the Son of God,
> who is himself God, must be the highest provocation"
> (Tong).

What does a man do when he treads the Son of God underfoot? He denies that Jesus of Nazareth was really the Son of God. He scorns the authority of Christ. He deserts the church and, in effect, causes some of the brethren of Christ to fall. He may even join those who persecute God's people. He undermines the kingdom of God, makes a mockery of the gospel of Christ. He stamps out the voice of his conscience, stifles the pleading of the Spirit of God, stubbornly turns his back on the sufferings of the Lord. When they fall into sin, people may wound the Son of God, and yet on repentance be freely pardoned and welcomed back into his love. But this is worse: this is a man who has seen Calvary's love, experienced Calvary's blessing, yet despite that, has scornfully spat upon the Lamb of God, turned aside from the cross, and gone deep into the way of sin, caring nothing for the gospel or for God.

How shall such a person be brought again to repentance? What else remains for him but judgment?

And how can a Christian sink into such a fearful position? Simply by neglecting to worship God!

Punishment will fall upon all who profane the blood of the covenant.

There was a time when these wilful sinners had been sanctified by the blood of Christ: they had been made holy, and were consecrated to God's service. They had once believed that the blood of Jesus was sacred blood, shed to cleanse away their sins. They had once been purged by that blood. But now they have fallen so far from God, their hearts have become so hardened, that they consider Jesus to be no more than an ordinary man, they reckon his life to have no more value than their own. Once they had spoken of the blood of Christ in reverence; now they laugh at it in derision. To them the blood of Christ has become an unholy thing, an occasion for common blasphemy, a convenient curse.

Persisting in wilful sin inevitably leads to such moral decay, to such fathomless crime against the love of God. But let no one who still has reverence for the blood of Christ, who still believes in him as the Son of God and the eternal Saviour, think themselves included in this condemnation. Just take warning lest the time should come when these verses *do* describe your state.

Is it possible for a Christian to come into this condition? It is! And that *simply by* neglecting to worship God!

Punishment will fall upon those who scorn the gracious Spirit.

It is dreadful to despise the Son of God. It is more dreadful, and shows a greater hardness of heart, to scorn the blood of Christ, and to call that precious blood a common thing. But those two are blasphemy against the Son of God, from which, Jesus said, a sinner might turn in repentance, and find pardon.

But now we come to blasphemy against the Holy Spirit, which shows a heart so hardened by sin that repentance is impossible. Why? Because the Holy Spirit alone can bring a person under conviction of sin, quicken faith in the blood of Christ, and so make pardon possible. But if the hardened soul despises the whisper of the Holy Spirit, if it derides the grace of God, how shall it then be brought to salvation? For that person "there remains no further sacrifice for sins." If people outrage the Spirit of God, who is sent by God to impart grace to the sinful heart, how will they find grace? But if they do not find grace, then they must abide under the law, which will stand up against them on the day of judgment.

Who will plead the cause of such blasphemers? None! for they have crushed their only Advocate underfoot, crucified him afresh, put him to death, nullified his grace.

Inexorably the wrath of God must bear down upon them, and how sore will be their punishment!

That is why Jesus said:

> *"I tell you solemnly that all kinds of sin and blasphemy can be pardoned; but someone who blasphemes against the Holy Spirit cannot be pardoned. Whoever speaks a word against the Son of man, it will be forgiven. But if anyone speaks against the Holy Spirit, it will never be forgiven - not in this world nor in the world to come"* (Mt 12a:31-32).

So there are people who once knew the Son of God, were once cleansed in the blood of Christ, once received grace from the Holy Spirit, but grossly abused the mercy they received by turning, like the sow, back to their filth, or, like the dog, back to their vomit (Pr 26:11; 2 Pe 2:22). If they insolently ignore the wooing of the Spirit who would draw them back to Christ, the time will certainly come when the Lord will no longer strive with them. How will they then be restored to repentance and faith?

There is no way it can be done, for there is no other sacrifice for sins. How can a Christian fall into this state of ruin? Simply by neglecting to worship God! Therefore -

*"Do not forsake the assembling of yourselves together,
which some have turned into a habit. Rather, you should
exhort each other with growing urgency as you see the
Day approaching" (vs. 25)*

If a man or woman despised the law of Moses, they were put to death
"without mercy" - no sympathy, no pity, no kindness, was allowed. But
then it speaks of a "much worse punishment". But what could be worse
than to die without mercy? Surely to die within mercy, to die despite
mercy! If a man broke the word of Moses, he offended the *justice* of
God. But when a man breaks the word of Jesus, he offends the *grace* of
God. What do you suppose, then: shall he not be thought worthy of much
sorer punishment? How much sorer? He does not say. You may imagine
that for yourself

THE RECOMPENSE

*"For we know the One who said, `Revenge is mine, and
I will surely take it;' and again, `The Lord will judge his
people.' It is a terrible thing to fall into the hands of the
living God!"*

"We know him" - so there is nothing secret about the judgments of God.
It is revealed to all who make an effort to see, both by reason and by
revelation. Every person who is able to think may become aware of God
and of his wrath against sin. A line or two earlier (vs. 29) the apostle had
asked them: "what do you think?" Just reason it out for yourself. No
great wit is required to recognise the inevitability of the coming
judgment. Therefore no one has any reasonable excuse for turning away
from God -

*"For God's anger is pouring out of heaven against
human ungodliness and against those people who in
their unscrupulous wickedness hold back the truth. They
stand already condemned because the knowledge of God
has not been hidden in a corner; rather, the Lord has
shown himself to them quite plainly. How has he done
that? Through the physical creation: for the invisible
attributes of God - his limitless power and his divine
nature - are made clearly visible in the world of nature
around us. Therefore any who denies God will be left
speechless in the hour of judgment" (Ro 1:18-20).*

If people who have never heard of Christ are bereft of excuse and face divine wrath, how much more will God's anger blaze against those who do know the Saviour, yet fail to walk righteously? Nothing could be plainer than the words of

Jesus in this respect -

> *"Any slave who knows his lord's will, but fails to be ready on time, or disobeys his master, will be lashed many times. But if the slave acted in ignorance, not knowing he was doing wrong, he will receive only a few lashes. If people have been given much, from them much will be required; but if little has been entrusted to them, then little will be required from them" (Lu 12:47-48).*

Notice how God, to make our duty doubly clear, has also recorded it in writing. So if we may know the judgment of God by reason, then we may also know it by revelation, for it is written, "Revenge is mine!" and, "The Lord will judge his people."

"*Revenge is mine!*" Will anyone be able to rob God of his right of retribution? Will anyone say it is unjust of him to call people to account for their wicked deeds?

Since they have worked evil against God, it is simple justice for God to work judgment upon them - particularly if they wilfully reject the divine offer of mercy and salvation. When injury and offence have been piled against God, obstinately and deliberately, who can dispute his right to rise in indignation and punish such wrong-doers? God has the power to execute such vengeance, and in due course it will be revealed.

But note that vengeance is God's, who jealously guards the privilege. We dare not try to usurp it -

> *"Do not pay back anyone with hurt for hurt. Conduct yourself with perfect integrity in the sight of everyone. Exerting all your skill, do whatever you can to live peaceably with all your neighbours. Dearly beloved, never avenge yourselves; prefer rather to make room for God to act on your behalf. Is it not written: 'Revenge is mine, and I will surely take it,' says the Lord. Therefore if your enemy is hungry, feed him; if he is thirsty, give him something to drink. When you do that you will be heaping coals of fire upon his head! So do not let evil*

overcome you; instead, you should overcome evil with good" (Ro 12:17-21).

So then, we must not take personal revenge in any form at any time, no matter how great the provocation. But we are not defenceless, for the Lord himself promises to exact full retribution on our behalf, either in this world or in the world to come.

Therefore, if we show an enemy kindness and he responds only with further cruelty, we know that his action has been carefully noted by God; he will be fanning the flames of the fiery indignation of the Eternal Judge.

God's vengeance differs from ours, because it is based on a perfect knowledge of all circumstances. Therefore it is linked in scripture with the idea of *recompense* - that is, of punishment or reward proportional to behaviour -

"To me belong revenge and recompense ... The Lord will judge his people" (De 32:35-36).

"I will recompense" - that is, the Lord will render to each man an exact equivalent for his sins. This retaliation is pronounced upon everyone who rejects Christ. Those who trust in Christ may rejoice, for he made expiation for iniquity, and their sin is no longer reckoned to them. But those who deny Christ must be denied by him.

They will then have to come before God bearing the full load of their wrongdoing, affronting God with all the injury they have caused him and his people. What else can he do except requite them fully for it?

From all this the apostle concludes:

"It is a terrible thing to fall into the hands of the living God!"

Under the law of Moses, men were punished by human hands, which mitigated considerably the force of the punishment. But those who despise the grace of God will be punished by the "hands" of God, which must indeed be a dreadful thing. If those arms wield the lash, how shall it be borne? If those hands imprison the wicked, how shall they escape?

Is this not

"Poetic Justice, with her lifted scale,
Where, in nice balance, truth with gold she weighs.[51]"

The gentle hands that the blasphemer once ground under the iron heel of sin will become the remorseless hands of divine vengeance. Those nail-pierced hands reached out to them in love, yet they brushed them impatiently aside, scorning the grace of God. But in the hour of judgment those same hands, the hands of the God who can never die, the hands of the Judge who will never tire, will impose the punishment that can never end.

The warning, you should notice, was not given to people outside the church, but to those who were in it, yet were drifting away from it. The apostle was not preaching a gospel sermon to the unsaved when he declared how terrible it is to fall into the hands of God. He was warning saints against backsliding. God grant that its threat never falls upon you or me. Only cling to Jesus and it never will.

---

[51] Alexander Pope (1688-1744), **The Dunciad**, Book One, lines 52,53.

Chapter Eleven:

PATIENCE AND FAITH

The 16th century Earl of Southampton was a connoisseur of fine literature. Accordingly, the poet Edmund Spenser decided to seek the earl's opinion of his newly completed romantic epic, The Faerie Queen. From the very first page Southampton's delight began to mount, and he soon commanded one of his servants: "Go bear Master Spenser a gift of twenty pounds" - a large sum in those days. The earl returned to the romance, and after a few more pages the beauty of the poetry incited him to call the servant again: "Go bear Master Spenser another twenty pounds."

Reading still further, and entranced beyond measure, he cried out a third time: "Go turn that fellow out of my house, for I shall be ruined if I read further![52]"

I do not suppose you have found the foregoing pages as enchanting as the earl found Spenser's poem. Yet I hope you are at least eager to read on; for we are nearly at the end of our quest, and some of the best is yet to come.

We have looked at the remonstrance, the reason, and the recompense; and now two items remain -

THE REMEMBRANCE

"Never forget those early days, just after you were enlightened, when you suffered so much. You struggled bravely against fierce opposition. And you endured a double burden: for either you were exposed to public ridicule and violence; or you stood shoulder to shoulder with those who were being abused. But you kept on helping those who were in prison, and remained cheerful even when your own goods were roughly seized. You did

---

[52] You will find a sonnet by Spenser at the end of this chapter.

this because you knew that in heaven you have possessions that are richer and indestructible" (He 10:32-34).

Recollection of the experiences of days gone by can be a great means of preventing apostasy. He asks them to remember that they had once been "enlightened" - "translated from the kingdom of darkness to the kingdom of God's dear Son." But we have been illuminated so that we might illuminate. To slip back into darkness frustrates the purpose of God. How shall he tolerate such folly? He is God, the living God, the unchanging God: it is ridiculous for us, who are the dust of the earth, to pit ourselves against the Lord, the Everlasting Creator.

The apostle asks them to remember two things -

REMEMBER YOUR FORMER TROUBLES

They had *"endured"* with admirable patience, and with extraordinary fortitude they had withstood all attempts to draw them away from Christ. They had quietly borne the greatest suffering, continuing in severe distress without complaint. Their enemies had bullied them to renounce Christ. But with patient resignation and abiding confidence in God, they had triumphed.

How they had struggled! Only by a mighty effort, striving desperately against numerous antagonists, had they overcome. They had contended earnestly for the faith; they had laboured hard for the gospel; they had fought successfully against all adversity. Would they now annul those brave efforts by falling away?

During that dreadful trial, undergoing hardship and pain, they had prevailed over countless difficulties. What losses they had suffered! What calamity they had experienced! How prolonged and weary the test of faith had been! But they were through it all. A time of peace had come. Yet now they were falling away!

Here is an amazing thing: many will stand fast for God when persecution rages fierce and strong; yet when all is peaceful they become careless, drift away from the church, fall back into sin, and risk final condemnation! Hence the ever needful exhortation: *"never stop going to church!"* (He 10:25).

Some of their former trials are especially noted by the apostle -

They were afflicted in themselves

Just as Paul had experienced (1 Co 4:9), so they too had been *"exposed to public ridicule"* - the word suggests a mob of buffoons, a circus show, shambling clowns. The early Christians were dragged into the arenas of the Romans, clothed in weird garments, sexually assaulted under the mocking gaze of the mob, fed to wild animals, used as living torches to illuminate garden parties, subjected to every insult, abuse and distress.

They were afflicted in their reputations

Compelled to bear reproach, branded as barbarians, thieves, law-breakers, their name slandered, their honour smirched, afflicted with shame, and made objects of infamy, they bore the scandal of every kind of disgrace. A man may bravely abide physical suffering; but if you reproach his good name, soil his honour, or degrade his high principle, he may find those contempts much harder to bear. But all this and more they had borne patiently and well.

They were afflicted in their brethren

Even when they were not themselves being persecuted, yet they boldly linked themselves with others who were. They did not hide away, hoping no one would discover that they were Christians; instead they openly avowed both their allegiance to Christ and their support of his people. They claimed fellowship with those who were being maltreated. They made the trials of others their own trials. They did not shirk the responsibility given them to help each other, whether in pleasure or pain.

Thus Christians should always be: not selfish, but willing to share in the sorrows of others, as well as their blessings. We should be to each other true companions, as well in persecution as in peace; having compassion for each other, being one in sympathy and fellow-feeling. Are we not brothers and sisters in Christ? Are we not all members of the one society, parts of the same body (Ro 12:4-5).

REMEMBER YOUR FORMER CONFIDENCE

They gladly allowed their goods to be plundered, and stood calmly by while their property and belongings were confiscated. Openly and violently the looters had attacked them, snatching away everything they had, roughly stripping them of all their possessions. They had no protection from the law, no opportunity for redress, no possibility of regaining their stolen goods. Left naked, poverty stricken, ravaged, subject to every kind of indignity and grief, still they remained *"joyful"*. The apostle marvelled because they had accepted such awful rapine *"cheerfully"* - almost with great delight!

Truly God had answered in them the apostle's prayer that all the saints everywhere might be *"strengthened mightily, according to God's glorious power, so that they might possess unshakeable endurance, patience, and joyfulness!"* (Cl 1:11).

There are many who know how to be patient. There are some who have learnt to be long suffering. But how many are there who couple these things with *"joyfulness"*?

However, this is the standard required by the Lord: that we learn how to accept calmly all kinds of hardship, persevering in faith, patience, and forbearance, and that we do it gladly!

Are you willing to reach that standard? Then call upon the Lord for it to be done. His mighty strength will be made available to you for this very purpose, as surely as it was in Bible days.

Those early Christians were able to show such amazing fortitude and forbearance because, as the apostle reminded them, "you knew that in heaven you have possessions that are richer and indestructible." Treasures were promised them in Christ far beyond what their enemies had stolen.

So there is an inner consciousness, a deep assurance, a certain calm knowledge, that a real Christian has that no amount of persecution can harm. Perhaps this is the greatest of all prizes that we have received by God's grace. It is certainly one that nothing on earth can destroy.

So we read of the manner in which God has given us

> *"the riches that come from fully understanding and fully believing the gospel" (Cl 2:2);*

> *and again, "Though I may suffer ... yet I am not ashamed; for I know in whom I have believed, and I am persuaded that he will safely keep everything I have put into his hands until that coming Day" (2 Tim 1:12).*

Those who have this inward persuasion can echo the confidence of Peter -

> *"Beloved, you should not think it strange when you are tested by a fiery trial, as if something out of order were happening to you. Rather you should rejoice, because now you can share in Christ's sufferings; which means that when his glory is revealed you will experience unbounded, rapturous joy"[53] (1 Pe 4:12-13).*

Constantly then we are exhorted to remember that in heaven there awaits the faithful Christian greater wealth than anyone has ever dreamed of - a mansion built by the Father's own hand, garments that never wear out, pleasures that never pall, possessions that will bring gladness for ever. Keeping this vision before the eye is a great means of preventing apostasy. So let us gaze upon it a little more -

THE REWARD

THERE IS THE REWARD OF CONFIDENCE

> *"Don't cast away your confidence, for it promises a wonderful reward" (He 10:35)*

The Greek word translated "confidence" is interesting –

It means "all outspokenness"

> *"Some of those who came from Jerusalem asked, 'Isn't this the man they are wanting to find and kill? Yet here he is speaking boldly and no-one is doing anything about it!" (Jn 7:25-26a)*

Though under threat of death, Jesus spoke the message of God openly and bluntly.

---

[53] Note how those words of Peter are relevant to our present consideration, for he spoke them against the background of the judgment of God that must begin at the House of God, vs 17-18. He concluded: "Therefore let everyone who suffers according to the will of God keep on doing good, and commit your lives into his hand, for he is your Creator and deserves your trust" (vs. 19).

Likewise Paul, although he was already in prison because of his preaching, craved even more boldness to proclaim Christ -

> *"Pray for me, so that I will always know just what to say; then when I preach the mystery of the gospel, I will be able to do so more boldly than ever before. I am an ambassador in chains. Therefore I should speak up and speak out. Your prayers will help me to do it" (Ep 6:19-20)*

The apostles in Jerusalem also scorned the warnings of the Jews and begged God for greater zeal and courage -

> *"Now Lord, you have heard all their threats. So because we are your servants we ask you to help us to declare your word with greater boldness. And when they had finished praying, the place where they were gathered shook like an earthquake. They were all filled with the Holy Spirit and proclaimed the word of God "openly" (Ac 4:29,31)*

Then Paul wrote again to the Corinthians:

> *"I will speak about you with great boldness, for you fill me with pride, and bring me great comfort; despite all our troubles, you make me full of joy" (2 Co 7:4)*

Those references show that the apostle was exhorting the Hebrew Christians not to allow persecution to soften their fearless preaching of the gospel. Such plain and zealous preaching will attract a great reward on that Day.

It means "frankness"

That is, plain speech, candid, open, free of reserve, disguise, or duplicity.

When Jesus talked about his coming sufferings and death, it says, "He spoke about it openly" (Mk 8:32) - he did not hesitate to give out all of God's truth, even though he knew it would offend some; and, in fact, Peter "took him aside to rebuke him! How different was the attitude of the people: "No one dared to speak openly about him, because they were afraid of the Jews" (Jn 7:13).

The meaning of the word in this use is shown in John 18:20 -

> *"Jesus replied, 'I speak "openly" to the world. I have always taught in places where the Jews frequently gather ... My teaching has never been conducted in secret."*

How powerful the testimony of the church would be if this could be said of every preacher: "he spoke openly to the world; he always taught where the people had resort; he hid none of the counsel of God!" There was a time when these Hebrews had practised such bold preaching; but now they were in danger of losing this confidence, and with it the reward of God.

Hold fast then to your confidence, and be frank in your witness for Christ.

It means "bluntness".

Good preaching is plain and sincere preaching, forthright and determined. When he wrote about the abolition of the law of Moses, and in a few sentences shattered the ancient economy, branding it a *"ministry of death"*, Paul described it as *"the letter that kills"* - which was brave enough. But then, speaking about the glorious gospel, Paul said, "Because we have such a marvellous hope, we speak out vigorously" (2 Co 3:12). Forcefully, bluntly, he pressed home the claims of the gospel, and insisted that people should forsake the old way and entirely conform their lives to the new.

How desperately in our day we need men and women who plainly, sincerely, strongly present to the people the claims of holiness, godliness, sobriety and righteousness. That is the kind of preaching that will excite a great reward. It means "assurance"

That is, as members of God's royal priesthood with full right of access to the throne of grace :

> let us approach God with spirit and energy
>
> let us be courageous in faith
>
> let us be daring in believing for great things
>
> let us be free from timidity caused by guilt
>
> let us have no shame in prayer
>
> let us have simple trust in the promise of God

let us be fairly persuaded of the mercy of God

let us have full confidence in the grace of God

let us have a certain expectation of his blessing

let us have the utmost assurance of his goodness

let us have an undoubting steadiness of mind.

And this great boldness of faith is not reserved for an elect few, but is the rightful possession of every child of God. It comes to us freely in conjunction with our faith in the Saviour -

> *"By Christ Jesus our Lord, and because of our faith in him, we dare to have boldness before God, confidently claiming open access into his presence. We do this without any anxiety, for he allows us the privilege of free and unrestricted approach to his throne!" (See Ep 3:12.)*

The apostle John also delighted in this word -

> *"If we keep close to Christ we will be able to meet him with confidence, and without shame, when he comes" (1 Jn 2:28) ...*

> *If we love one another, then with a clear conscience and* complete confidence *we will be able to approach God" (3:18-21) ...*

> *"Because love has come to perfection among us we can face the Day of Judgment with the utmost confidence" (4:13-17) ...*

> *"Whenever we are in agreement with God's will, then we can approach with absolute confidence, knowing that he will listen to us" (5:14-15).*

So we are left in no doubt that God wants us to approach him with confidence! The whole could be summed up in these words: "We should have a calm assurance of the full trustworthiness of God; a firm belief in the reality of his power; a perfect reliance upon the integrity of his Word."

Therefore he says, "Don't throw your confidence away!" The Greek verb translated "throw away" occurs only twice in the NT. It means "to discard, lose, cast off". So there are many who carelessly lose their confidence by ignoring the means of gaining that confidence. And there are others who fling it away, choosing to abandon their trust in God. Vow never to do such a thing, he says, because your confidence toward God is the only link you have with the heavenly treasure. So then hold fast to your confidence, because it will bring a glorious reward.

The Lord will give you an enormous return of good for all the evil you have suffered. He will repay with vast increase whatever you have rendered him in faithful service. And you should hold fast to your confidence, because it is the only channel through which God can recompense you for your sacrifice.

Here is God's desire: to return to every one of his children a full equivalent of all they have given him in service. He promises full compensation for every loss they have suffered for his sake - and then he plans to add an exceedingly generous reward!

See the absolute completeness of Christ's atonement on our behalf. Suppose the Father had done nothing for us. We were so deeply in debt to him that not centuries of toil could have cleared us of its burden. But in one sacrifice Jesus paid the whole bill, cancelled the entire account. Now, so long as we maintain our trust in Christ, we may labour for God as willing servants, and for that service, he will give us due payment. But so great is his grace, so magnificent his kindness, that he declines to pay us mere wages, and insists upon increasing our hire by a glittering bonus.

We may well praise him with unending praise! But all this is true, and can be effective, only as we hold fast to our confidence in Christ. Cast away that confidence and the whole of our staggering debt to God must appear again. Where then will be the possibility of reward?

THERE IS THE REWARD OF PATIENCE

"After you have done the will of God, then you will need patience while you wait for his promise to be fulfilled. And it will not be long. He who is coming, will come; he won't be late!" (He 10:36-37).

Impatience is the cause of many throwing aside their confidence. We have need of patience!

"Patience is an high virtue!" (Chaucer)

"Patience is the best remedy for every trouble." (Plautus)

"He that has patience may compass anything." (Rabelais)

"How poor are they that have not patience!" (Shakespeare)

"Those who have no patience will have nothing." (English Proverb)

"Nothing you do will succeed without patience." (Japanese Proverb)

"Patience is bitter, but its fruit is sweet." (Japanese Proverb)

"Where there is patience, everything is possible." (Maltese Proverb)

"Patience is the best prayer." (Hindi Proverb)

What is patience?
Many confuse resignation with patience.

Resignation is lifeless, but patience is living. Resignation is a conquered submission to the will and authority of another, without hope of change. Resignation is slavery, patience is freedom. Patience refers to the quietness of one's mind, the self-possession of one's spirit:

> Patience is the ability to suffer provocation with unruffled temper.

> Patience is being able to endure heavy calamity without murmuring.

> Patience is knowing how to accept toil and trouble without fretfulness.

> Patience will bear evils and offences without discontent.

> Patience will accept injury without retaliation.

> Patience is prepared to wait long for promised good.

> Patience knows that justice will be done, that right will prevail.

> Patience will suffer any affliction with unwavering fortitude.

Patience cannot be provoked, neither is it revengeful.

Patience is not hasty, nor over-eager, nor impetuous.

most of all, in the thought of our present text: Christian patience shows constant perseverance in the pursuit of good.

After the will of God is done, patience enables one to wait calmly, without discontent, confidently expecting the promised reward to appear. The literal meaning of the Greek word is "cheerful and hopeful endurance, coupled with constancy of purpose." Cheerfulness, hopefulness, endurance, constancy - all are essential elements of Christian patience. If your patience lacks these, it will fall short of the promised reward. At all times, then, we should be

- *cheerful:* relying on the present help of God
- *hopeful*: expecting the promised blessing of God.
- *steadfast*: trusting in the future reward of God.
- *constant*: committed to the perfect will of God.

We need patience, especially, after we have done the will of God. What is the will of God? Each must discover that for himself; but whatever it may be, we need to discover it, do it, and then, with cheerful, hopeful patience, wait for the promised reward.

To this end we should echo the prayer of the psalmist -

> *"Teach me your will, O God, and how to do it, for you are my God. Let your gracious Spirit keep me from straying into enemy territory. For your own name's sake, renew my life and strength, O Lord" (Ps 143:10-11).*

May God then deliver us from impatience - that spirit of uneasiness, of petulance, of fretfulness - that restless desire for change - that sense of frustration when we experience delay - that intolerance of trials. May the Lord save us from being hasty, and from showing anger at restraint; may he keep us from peevishness and irritability. For, if the Lord will keep us free from these things, if he will show us his will, if he will help us to do it, and to be patient, then we shall surely *"receive the promise."*

For their further encouragement, the apostle takes up two sayings from the Old Testament (vs 37-38). They are both found in Habakkuk 2:2-4. Here is the first of them -

> *"The Lord spoke to me and said: `Write down what you have seen; write it on tablets clearly enough for someone who is running past to read it. The vision waits for its proper time of fulfilment; but it will speak in the end, and will prove to be true. Though it seems to delay, keep on waiting for it, for it will come at the right time; it will not be late" (Ha 2:2-3).*

God has seen to it that his promises are written down. They are written down plainly. They are written down so plainly that even a person harried by constant trouble, pressed by constant activity - who, as it were, has opportunity to do no more than run past the tablets - may yet read them and understand them

Or perhaps the translation should have said this: the promises of God and the warnings of God are so plainly written that the directions they give are entirely clear. People reading them may instantly set their lives accordingly and, escaping the judgments, run into the haven of God's love.

But there is an appointed time for every vision to be accomplished, every promise to be fulfilled. Therefore know that there is no lie or shadow of turning with God. In the end, his word will triumph, his voice will speak, the miracle will be wrought.

If you have prayed the prayer of faith, then stand fast, hold to your confidence: though the promised answer is delayed, it will surely come. Wait for it then in cheerful patience. From the moment you prayed, the answer started coming and, in a while - what is in fact a very little while - it will reach you, nothing can delay it beyond God's time, nothing can prevent it from being accomplished. That is, nothing except *impatience*, which may force you to cast aside your confidence. But, if you wait, it will come.

The second advent of Christ is particularly in mind here. Sometimes we feel that God has forgotten man, that he has left the human race to destroy itself. We ask, "What hinders his coming? Why is he so long in appearing?" But what seems a long time to us is a little time to God (2 Pet 3:3-4,8-9). To the sinner, to the ungodly, to Satan - Christ will come all too quickly!

Sometimes we think heaven is slow. But we should trust God. While he may seem slow according to our concept of time, he is far from being so. It is quite clear: God never delays his promise unnecessarily; he is not tardy in honouring his word; he is not slow in fulfilling his obligations. But he is extraordinarily kind, and earnestly longs that not one soul should perish, but that all should be saved. As quickly as it is good, and profitable, and well for your soul, so quickly will God send you his promise.

THERE IS THE REWARD OF FAITH

"Now the just shall live by faith; but if anyone pulls back I will no longer find any pleasure in him. But we do not belong among those who fall away into damnation. We are among those who believe, and so gain the salvation of their souls" (He 10:38-39).

We now meet with the second quotation from Habakkuk: "The just shall live by faith."

"THE JUST"

That is, "the righteous man". This then is the principle by which a righteous man may be known. This is the principle by which we must live if we would be righteous: Faith.

One of the first principles of faith is humility - as Habakkuk shows: "The ungodly are swollen with pride; their souls are crooked; but the just shall live by faith." This is an unchangeable law of God: the humble and trusting heart alone is acceptable to heaven. This alone enables a person to stand uprightly before God, cleansed of all corruption; this alone enables a man or woman to walk according to the will of God and to merit the reward of God. So it says that the just

"SHALL LIVE"

None apart from the just are really able to live, in the fullest sense of the word. An unjust person is "dead even if he seems to be alive" (1 Ti 5:6). But those who are made righteous by faith and continue by faith will *live* - that is, they will remain in existence; death no longer has any power over them; they will continue for ever; they will never perish.

Yet they are also alive now: able to make the most out of life and to derive the greatest possible pleasure from the things of each day. In them dwell the grace and goodness of God. So they enjoy life, abundant life, eternal life, for they are earnest in godliness, active in righteousness, and happy in holiness. This is life: to KNOW God, to LOVE GOD, and to LIVE for God.

But only the righteous can know such "life", and even they only as they live

"BY FAITH"

There are many kinds of faith. Which one is meant here? Simply that faith which stems from a strong conviction that God is the Father of all, and that it is our privilege and duty to serve God wholeheartedly.

This quality of faith results in a burning zeal for godliness, and an intense desire to please God. It is faith founded on a clear hope of the return of Christ, and a solemn certainty of the judgment that faces the ungodly. This faith knows that human wilfulness will result in the wrath of God, but that human righteousness will result in the reward of God. It is faith that has measured the promise of God, found it to be full of delight, and therefore presses forward to receive that promise.

Such faith as this brings pleasure to God. But that pleasure soon turns to displeasure if the believer becomes a backslider (He 10:38).

How does a person "draw back"? We "draw back" when we hold our faith out of sight. Faith to be livable has to be open. If we cower before persecution, or shrink from our duty, then we become guilty of "drawing back".

The meaning of the word is clear in the following passages -

> *Paul said to the elders of the church, "I kept back nothing that was beneficial for you"(Ac 20::20); and again, "I never shrank away from declaring to you the whole counsel of God" (vs. 27).*

Its meaning is seen also in the unhappy example of Peter on one occasion: "Before the delegates came from James, Peter ate with the gentiles. But after the messengers arrived he withdrew, separating himself from the Romans because he was afraid of what the Jews might say" (Ga 2:12).

Should you or I, through fear, desert the cause of God and separate ourselves from the people of God, then God would consider us backsliders and no longer find any pleasure in us.

Let us make sure, then, that we are not among those who draw back, for their end is "perdition" - eternal ruin, everlasting loss, unending misery. Those who draw back are put into the same category as Judas and the ungodly: for Judas is the "*son of perdition*" (Jn 17:12); and the destiny of the ungodly is "destruction and perdition" (1 Ti 6:9); and Peter speaks of "the perdition of the ungodly" (2 Pe 3:7).

But how could we be numbered amongst such company? By the grace of God we have learned to cleave to God. Our faith is in Christ: we rely on his promise; we trust in his mercy; and we are confident that we have received eternal life.

Having believed, let us live by faith. For if we live by faith and die in faith, our souls will be safe forever.

Chapter Twelve:

ENTHRONED WITH CHRIST

The Roman historian Quintus Curtius[54] tells the following story about Alexander the Great -

> "It chanced that a Macedonian common soldier, hardly able to stand up and hold his weapons, had nevertheless reached the camp. On seeing him the king (Alexander), although he himself was just then warming himself beside a fire, leaped up from his chair, and taking his armour from the exhausted and hardly conscious soldier, bade him sit in his own seat. For a long time the man did not realise where he was resting nor by whom he had been rescued. At last, when he had recovered his vital heat and saw the royal seat and the king, he arose in terror. Alexander, looking kindly at him, said: `Do you understand, soldier, how much better a life you all have under a king than the Persians have? For with the Persians, to have sat in the king's seat would have been a capital crime, with you it has saved your life.'"

Those were happier days, when Alexander was still democratically minded. In later years he assumed ever more of the trappings of an oriental despot[55].

However, when I first read that story I at once saw the analogy between Alexander's grace to his weary soldier and the gift of Christ. Far more truly than the Macedonian conqueror could say it, Christ has "saved our lives" by bringing us into the holiest and sitting us upon his throne.

Yet many Christians remain like that terrified soldier, appalled at the prospect of such dizzying honour, unable to believe such good news. So

---

[54] Curtius composed his history circa 50 A.D. I have lost the details of the book from which the above translation of the Latin text was taken.

[55] Remember my comment on ancient monarchs in the first chapter.

to conclude this book, let us look at one of the most sensational statements in all of Paul's letters. Here he tells us, not merely that God has invited us in Christ to approach his throne without fear, but that he has actually lifted us higher and *seated us upon the throne*! -

"God has raised us up with Christ and enthroned us with him in the heavenlies[56]

"Enthroned with Christ" - what does that vivid expression mean?

It is a colourful way of saying that God has given us access through Christ to all that belongs to his heavenly throne. The authority and the riches of that throne are available to us as though we were already and actually sitting on it in heaven. No event in the future can give us any more right to the throne than we now possess.

Even the resurrection will do no more than bring us into visible contact with the throne; it cannot add anything to the unassailable legitimacy of the claim we have already on all that the throne represents.

What *does* his throne represent for us?

The throne of God means the might and right that God possesses to do all that lies within his will. If we are seated upon the throne in Christ, then to us also, when we are doing the will of God, belong that same might and right. No one who sits upon that throne, who knows what it means and who utilises its wealth, can fail to triumph. Defeat overtakes us only when we dethrone ourselves through unbelief or disobedience.

Whatever the will of God for your life may be: prosperity or persecution; fame or obscurity; vast achievement or small; plenty or famine; city or desert; life or death - in every circumstance, under any condition, so long as you identify yourself with Christ upon the throne you cannot be other than truly rich and wholly invincible.

You may say, "But I am not in heaven, I am not sitting on a throne. I am here on earth, beset by all kinds of difficulties and infirmities." True. But that takes us to a consideration of one of God's highest gifts to us in Christ -

[56] Ep 2:6, translated in its dynamic sense.

A ROYAL PREROGATIVE

A king retains all his royal prerogatives even when he is absent from his palace, perhaps visiting some far distant part of his empire. Many monarchs in the past were obliged to spend years at a time away from their palaces, leading their armies into battle. There on the frontiers of empire, they lived in rude hardship among their troops. Yet they remained emperors, their authority no less absolute, nor their wealth in any way diminished. For a time, to suit the purposes of war, they were content to live poorly and to suffer the rigours of battle; yet not for a moment did they hesitate to call themselves "king". During their long separation from the throne, they continued to call upon all resources inherent in their title; they boldly grasped whatever they needed to win their wars and to enforce their rule.

AMBASSADORS FOR CHRIST

A similar idea is contained in Paul's comparison of a Christian with an ambassador (2 Co 5:20). An ambassador represents his home government in a foreign country. His power to affect what happens in that country depends entirely upon the power of his home land. If he represents a feeble nation, while his embassy is among a mighty people, then his influence will be small. But if the position is reversed, then he will, of course, have immense influence.

Here is wonderful encouragement! For we represent the government of the King of kings and the Lord of lords, an empire whose expansion will never end! (Is 9:7). None dare withstand the will of our King. In fact, no one "can" withstand it! Whatever he pleases he does, in heaven and on earth (Ps 115:3; Is 35:6). It is a pleasant thing to serve such a mighty Lord! As his royal ambassadors, we should know that whatever we speak in his name, expressing his will, with a firmness that brooks no denial, must surely be done!

There is an illustration of this in the annals of ancient Rome. It describes one of the most extraordinary incidents in the history of embassies. I have put together the following account from the writings of Polybius and Livy[57]. It is also a remarkable instance of fulfilled prophecy, for Daniel[58] foresaw the even in his oracle about the "King of the North" -

A TOUGH ENVOY

In the year 175 B.C. Antiochus IV became lord of the Seleucid Empire. A hugely successful monarch, he brought order to his kingdom, expanded its borders, and increased its wealth. He prospered so well that he began to think himself more than human. Surely no mere man could possess such riches and power? Surely he must be a son of the gods? So he proclaimed himself *"Epiphanes"* - the Shining One, the Manifestation of a god on earth. What could now be impossible for him? He conceived the vaulting ambition of conquering Egypt, and of adding to his dominions the splendours of the ancient empire of the Pharaohs.

So, near the end of the second century before Christ, Antiochus IV Epiphanes marched his legions into the land of the Nile. Pharaoh was no match for him, and Egypt began to crumble before his onslaught. City after city fell, until at last only one stronghold remained to defy him - the great city of Alexandria, at the mouth of the river. Antiochus ordered his army and his navy to advance. So long as Alexandria stood, Egypt could not be his.

In desperation the Alexandrians sent an urgent message across the Mediterranean, to the Roman senate, pleading for help.

The senators, hearing that Antiochus had become master of Egypt and very nearly of Alexandria also, were much alarmed. They disliked the idea of such a powerful

---

[57] See Polybius 29:2,27; Livy 44:19; 45:12,13.

[58] See Daniel 11:29-32. The fulfilment of the oracle, quoting Daniel's words, is described in 1 Maccabees 1:20-24, 54-64.

empire developing in the east and south. They decided to act swiftly. But they did not declare war on Antiochus, nor did they call up their mightiest legions nor summon their great fleet. Instead, the senate was content to bring out of retirement an elderly civil servant, by the name of Gaius Popilius Laenas. Him they despatched with a small guard of soldiers in three ships, to confront Antiochus at Alexandria.

Popilius was an arrogant man, renowned for his harsh temper. But across many years he had served Rome well, both as a former consul, and upon several missions as an envoy. Once again he was designated Rome's ambassador, and instructed to turn Antiochus back, or to declare war against him in the name of the Roman senate.

Popilius landed at Alexandria to find that Antiochus had pitched camp about 6 kilometres distant from the city, near the beach, with his powerful fleet moored just off-shore. At an appointed time, the two men approached each other across the sand. The king greeted Popilius courteously from a distance, and as they drew nearer to each other held out his hand to the Roman. But Popilius ignored both the greeting and the outstretched hand. Instead he abruptly gave Antiochus two tablets containing the senate's decree, with a stern instruction first to read it, and then, if he still chose to do so, to offer his hand in friendly welcome. Antiochus was surprised by this rough approach, but he took the tablets and read them with growing dismay. He announced to the envoy that he would discuss the decree with his advisors, and return with their reply on the morrow. But Popilius, showing his usual temper, acted with an arrogance that is still renowned! Because he was suffering from arthritis, which hindered him from crossing the beach, he had cut a stick cut from a vine. Now dragging the stick behind him, Popilius walked around Antiochus and drew a circle in the sand. Then he stepped back and said peremptorily: "You will give me your answer before you step out of that circle!"

Antiochus was at first struck dumb by this violent proceeding; but after hesitating a few moments he replied, "I will do what the senate decrees." He then led his army and navy back to Syria, deeply angered, bitterly complaining, but yielding to necessity. And on the way (as Daniel had seen nearly 400 years earlier) he vented his frustrated rage upon the helpless Jews.

What an amazing scene! There was Ephiphanes himself, the Divine Manifestation, with 50,000 soldiers behind him and a powerful fleet, confronting an arthritic and elderly Roman civil servant, who had only a handful of attendants. Yet the will of the envoy prevailed. The Shining One, despite his overwhelming might, despite his wrath at being treated so scornfully, had no choice but to retreat. Why? Because behind the envoy stood all the majesty of imperial Rome! Antiochus had once spent 14 years in Rome, as a hostage. He knew the awesome power of the Roman legions; he heard the crushing authority of the senate resounding in the voice of Popilius.

So he went off home sulking like a disobedient child. Later on, Antiochus sent his own envoys to the senate, with the message that peace with Rome had seemed preferable to any conquest (since it was the wish of the senate), and that Antiochus had obeyed the orders of the Roman envoys as if they had been gods. That was quite an admission from the man who called himself "Ephiphanes"!

DON'T STAND THERE BAFFLED!

We too are confronted by that old Shining One, Lucifer himself, proud, supported by demonic hordes. We stand alone on the sand, seemingly defenceless, helpless against our cunning and warlike foe. But we are ambassadors who have the Royal blood flowing through our veins. Our Father is the only King. His throne is already ours by right, along with all that belongs to his kingdom. The authority Popilius used so roughly was like thistle down in comparison with the limitless strength we have at our command!

But how would the Roman envoy have fared if he had cringed before Antiochus, snivelling with anxiety, timorous before the king's majesty? The proud and glittering monarch would have mocked the senate's decree, and then continued with his conquest of Egypt. Popilius would probably have been put to death at once, or at best would have been forced to return home a disgraced man.

So then when you are backed by the King's decree, when you are enforcing his purpose, when you are claiming his promise, you can and should speak with unyielding boldness. As certainly as Epiphanes himself had to treat the unarmed Roman legate as though he were a god, so will your spiritual foes be obliged to reckon with you as with God himself. Your voice is the voice of Christ. You have royal privileges. Speak them into existence by faith!

A RIGHTEOUS PROVISION

At this point someone may protest: "It may be true to say that some very good Christians are enthroned with Christ, and have great spiritual authority; but it cannot be true of me. I am too obviously sinful, too weak, too much full of doubt, too easily overthrown by temptation and by the devil. Despite my hardest struggles, I am defeated again and again. It is absurd for me to pretend that I am sitting on heaven's highest throne, or that I have any spiritual authority."

Away with such excuses! They are all demolished by one question -

ARE YOU DEAD OR ALIVE?

Let the Holy Spirit make these astonishing words real to you again -

> *"When you were dead in your sins, God made you alive together with Christ, and raised you up with him, and enthroned you with him in the heavenlies" (see Ep 2:4).*

When did God enthrone you with Christ in the heavenlies? Paul is emphatic: he did it when you were *dead*, absolutely dead in sin! You might think you are bad now, but you were worse *then*! You may not have gone far in righteousness, but you are certainly more advanced than you were *then*! However much you might now be defeated, you are not so broken as you were *then*!

At least you are now alive. Then you were wholly dead. But while you were in that state of utter spiritual death, God identified you with Christ; he united you with the Saviour's resurrection, ascension, and enthronement. How much more, then (since you now believe in Christ, and have discovered the power of the Holy Spirit, and have at least made a beginning in righteousness), must God now be willing to see you in the image of someone who is firmly identified with the enthroned Christ?

HOW DOES GOD ENTHRONE US?

Still someone might say: "That is a pretty theory; but how can it become real in practice? How can it affect my daily life? How can I actually experience the authority of the throne?"

The Lord brings this about in the same way he does everything: by the spoken word.

He simply declares it to be so; and it is. Then he expects us to declare it also, as people who believe that whatever God says is, is; and whatever he says is not, is not

This can be illustrated by the similar process that took place in the passion of Jesus, who was carried from righteousness to unrighteousness solely by the decree of God. Just as scripture says that we have been declared *righteous* by the word of God, so it also says that Jesus was declared *sinful* by the word of God (2 Co 5:21; etc). Now if God was able to reckon his sinless Son to be a *sinner*, then he can reckon this sinner, myself, to be *sinless*. In neither case does the reckoning rest upon human action, but only upon God's word. Nothing more is necessary. What God says is righteous, is righteous; what he says is unrighteousness, is unrighteousness.

Mark this: Jesus did not have to *do* any sin before the Father could reckon him *full* of sin; nor do you have to *do* anything righteous before the Father can reckon you *full* of righteousness. It is not a matter of our *doing* but of God's *reckoning*. If he was justly able to call Jesus a *sinner*, who had never done anything *sinful*, then he is justly able to call you *holy*, though you have never done anything *righteous*.

And see how powerful God's reckoning is! It is no mere abstraction. It is irresistible! Less than 24 hours after the word of sin was spoken, Christ was dead upon the cross. Yet how could that be? Does not scripture say that "*death is the wages of sin*"; and, "*a soul can die only if it sins*"? How then did he die, when he had done no iniquity? Simply because he was made a sinner, not by any action of his, but only by the divine decree. At once the penalty of sin was inescapably imposed upon him, which otherwise would have been impossible.

Still further, which is more difficult? To call an innocent man guilty, or to call a guilty man innocent? In the reckoning of law, the former is by far the heavier burden. Therefore, if the decree of God could bring guilt and death upon Jesus, much more easily can it bring innocence and life upon you and me.

But perhaps you will now say: "How is it then that I am not actually reigning in my daily life? How is it that my experience is still more like that of a slave than of a king? If the reckoning of God swiftly brought Jesus to the cross, why has that reckoning not brought me just as irresistibly to the throne?"

The answer lies in the fact that Christ himself had to co-operate with the Father in this process -

THREE VITAL STEPS

Accept the Father's Word

Jesus had to hear the word of the Father, believe it, and embrace it. He had to discover in scripture that the Father intended to reckon him sinful and to deal with him as a sinner. But having made that discovery, Jesus then had to be willing to activate the word of God by faith and to accept the inescapable consequence of death. This was surely the real source of his agony in the Garden of Gethsemane (Mt 26:36-44; Mk 14;32-36; Lu 22:41-44), and of his tortured cry, *"Let this cup pass from me!"*

It cannot be imagined that the Saviour shrank with such horror merely from the prospect of physical pain. Had he done so, he would have shown less courage than many of his own followers, including little children, who during the long, blood stained history of the church, have joyfully faced awful tortures for his sake.

Remember too, he himself had urged his disciples to rid themselves of any dread of suffering for the gospel. He taught them to face every torment with gladness, knowing that their reward in heaven would be great. Crucifixion was a terrible way to die; but thousands of Christian martyrs, strong men and gentle women alike, have bravely endured far more agonising deaths, often prolonged for many days, even many weeks. Clearly, Jesus could not have been afraid of the cross itself.

What then was he pleading with the Father to remove from him? Surely this awful sentence: *"Thou art a sinner! Therefore thou shalt die!"* He knew that the Father had resolved to reckon him a sinner. He also knew that God's reckoning would remain ineffectual until he embraced it by faith. He agonised in his pure soul against that terrible reckoning. Surely there was some other way? How deeply he loathed sin.

How sickening was its stench to his nostrils. How his flesh cringed from its foul touch. But the will of the Father remained resolute: "Unless you allow me to reckon you a sinner, and to bring death upon you, I will never be able to reckon so much as one of your brethren righteous and so bring life upon them!".

So Jesus yielded: "Father, let your will be done." He accepted the reckoning of God. He who knew no sin was made sin for us. The shadow of death crept over him.

Within 24 hours it was all over. His lifeless body was lying in the cold tomb. How powerful is the reckoning of God when it is believed!

Overcome Natural Reason

In the same way, righteousness and the throne became ours when we discover that the Father wants to reckon this upon each one of us, and when we wholly submit to that reckoning. Just as the reckoning of God was powerful to bring Christ to the cross, so it is powerful to bring us to the throne. Jesus' "sinlessness" could not thwart the divine reckoning; neither can your "sinfulness". But you must be willing to accept without reservation what God reckons to be so. And you will probably find this as hard to do as Jesus did, although in an opposite way.

This is the second point at which Christ had to co-operate with the reckoning of God. He had to overcome a natural and deep reluctance to accept the Father's declaration of sinfulness. Everything in him revolted against that horrifying word. He had never committed sin; how then could he become sin? He had to banish by fervent prayer this inner resistance to being reckoned a sinner and to receiving the penalty for sin.

So too, your carnal nature hates the idea of righteousness, and shrinks in rebellion from being declared righteous apart from any good deed of your own. The flesh loathes the gospel. Everything within you may cry out against the word of the Father: "How can I be called sinless when I am sinful? How can I be said to be on the throne when I am wallowing in dung? I "cannot" receive that word! I do not *want* to receive that word! I *will* not receive that word!"

But the flesh must be overcome, perhaps by your own Gethsemane. Just as Jesus struggled in prayer until he was able to receive the Father's word of sin, so you may need to struggle just as hard to receive the Father's word of righteousness. Not always, of course, for sometimes the word from heaven will drop into your spirit as softly and refreshingly as the falling dew. Nonetheless, whether easy or hard, until you do find God's promise, and believe it, it must remain ineffectual for you.

Stand Firm in Faith

Having embraced the reckoning of the Father, Christ then turned his face toward Calvary and the inescapable outworking of that word in his death and burial. Nothing on earth or in hell could then prevent the cross. His death became absolutely inevitable. When the Father's reckoning is believed and acted upon, is there any power in the entire universe that can even hope to thwart it?

If you are willing to believe and to act upon God's declaration that you are now his righteousness in Christ, then by the mighty reckoning of God you will be brought straight to the throne, and all its grace and glory will begin to break loose in your life. Sitting with Christ, serene in the heavenlies, you will lack nothing of the triumph of the cross, the joy of the resurrection, and the blessing of the ascension.

So then, abandon all attempts to "work" your way up to the throne. Take your stand there now, by faith, boldly seizing all that is rightly yours as God's gift to you in Christ.

A RIGOROUS PENALTY

Any person who claims authority over another must expect that authority to be tested. This is a universal principle, observable every day: at home, at work, in the church, wherever any kind of authority structure exists. Those over whom authority is claimed, whether they are young or old, will resist its exercise, and strive to maintain as much freedom as they can.

Likewise, if you claim spiritual authority, then pressure will inescapably be brought to bear upon it. Can you stand firm? Will you resist the enemy? Do you know how to maintain your authority against all attacks upon it?

Each Christian finally has only as much spiritual authority as he or she can hold under pressure, without panic, and without resorting to carnal strength.

Mark also how a bitter penalty is exacted from those who, having authority, fail to understand it or use it. How mercilessly their foes fall upon them. How tragic is their ruin! Employers who cannot maintain control over their workers will swiftly be brought to bankruptcy. School teachers who cannot control their pupils will soon experience the galling shame of a classroom in chaos. Parents who cannot control their children must expect a tragic harvest of delinquency. Have you been given authority? Then you had better learn what it is, and how to use it, or disgrace and desolation will overwhelm you.

CONCLUSION

Success in the service of God, then, is dependent upon knowing who you are in Christ, what authority God has given you, and then acting accordingly. Yet there are three cautions -

- suppose you abdicate the throne?
- suppose an enemy contests your claim?
- suppose you abuse your privileges?

We must cast aside those and all other challenges, and instead bravely grasp our God-given freedoms. Align yourself with God's opinion of you in Christ, and go on to serve him in true liberty and holiness, grasping all the privileges and fulfilling all the duties of his royal priesthood.

LAST WORD

I began the two previous chapters with an anecdote from the life of the renowned poet Edmund Spenser. Let me now end the book with one of his sonnets, in which the poet celebrates the resurrection of Christ and the wonder of his eternal love -

> Most glorious Lord of life! that on this day
>
> Didst make thy triumph over death and sin;
>
> And, having harrow'd hell, didst bring away
>
> Captivity thence captive, us to win:

This joyous day, dear Lord, with joy begin;

And grant that we, for whom thou didst die,

Being with thy dear blood clean washed from sin,

May live for ever in felicity!

And that thy love we weighing worthily,

May likewise love thee for the same again;

And for thy sake that all like dear didst buy,

With love may one another entertain:

So let us love, dear Love, like as we ought;

Love is the lesson which the Lord us taught[59].

---

[59] Sonnet #68.

BIBLIOGRAPHY

Against Heresies; Ante-Nicene Fathers; Vol. One; Eerdmans Publishing Co, Grand Rapids; 1979.

Believer's Bible Commentary; William Macdonald; Thomas Nelson Publishers; 1989.

Bible Background Commentary; Intervarsity Press, Nottingham UK; 1993.

Bible Knowledge Commentary, The; by John Walvoord and Roy Zuck; Cook Communications, Colorado Springs, Colorado; 1989.

Calvin's Commentaries; John Calvin (1509-1564).

College Press NIV Commentary, The; Joplin, Missouri; 1996.

Commentary on Ephesians, A; Charles Hodge (1797-1878).

Commentary on the Bible; Adam Clarke (1715-1832).

Commentary On The Old And New Testaments, A; John Trapp (1601-1669).

Commentary on the Old and New Testaments, A; Robert Jamieson, A. R. Fausset, David Brown; 1871.

Dunciad, The; Alexander Pope (1688-1744).

Explanatory Notes on the Whole Bible; John Wesley (1703-1791).

Exposition of the Entire Bible; John Gill (1690-1771).

Expositor's Bible Commentary, The; ed. Frank E. Gaebelein; Zondervan Publishers, GrandRapids, Michigan.

Expository Commentary; H.A. Ironside (1876-1951).

Great Religions of Modern Man, The; *Islam*; George Braziller, New York, 1962.

Histories, The; tr. by Aubrey de Selincourt and A. R. Burns; Penguin Books, London, 1972.

History of Christianity, A; Vol One; K. S. Latourette; Harper & Row, New York, 1975.

Holman New Testament Commentary; ed. Max Anders; B & H Publishing Group, Nashville, Tennessee; 2004.

Interpreter's Bible, The; Abingdon Press, New York; 1952.

IVP New Testament Commentary Series, The; Intervarsity Press, Nottingham, UK.

Jewish New Testament Commentary; David H. Stern; Jewish New Testament Publications, Inc., Clarksville, Maryland; 1982.

Matthew Henry's Commentary; Marshall, Morgan, and Scott, London; 1953.

Matthew Poole's Commentary; 1685

Nelson's New Illustrated Bible Commentary; Thomas Nelson Inc., New York; 1999.

New Testament Commentary; Baker's Publishing House, Grand Rapids, Michigan; 1987.

Notes on the Bible; Albert Barnes (1798-1870).

People's New Testament Commentary, The; B. W. Johnson; Word Search Corporation, Nashville, Tennessee; 2010.

People's New Testament, The; by B. W. Johnson; 1891.

Poor Man's Commentary On The Whole Bible, The; Robert Hawker; 1850.

Preacher's Commentary, The; Word Inc., Nashville, Tennessee; 1992.

Preacher's Outline and Sermon Bible; Word Search Corporation, Nashville, Tennessee; 2010.

Priesthood Of All believers, The; Cyril Eastwood; Epworth Press, London 1960.

Pulpit Commentary, The; ed. Joseph S. Exell, Henry Donald Maurice Spence-Jones; 1881.

Religio Medici; ed. C. A. Patrides Penguin Classics edition, 1977.

Royal Priesthood Of The Faithful, The; Cyril Eastwood; Epworth Press, London 1963.

Sensible Man's View of Religion, The; J. H. Holmes (1879-1964).

Vincent's Word Studies; Marvin R. Vincent; 1886

What Luther Says, compiled by Ewald M. Plass; Concordia Publishing House, St Louis, 1959.

Wiersbe's Expository Outlines; Warren W. Wiersbe; Publisher, David C. Cook, Colorado Springs, Colorado.

Word Pictures In The New Testament; A. T. Robertson; 1933.

World's Greatest Story, The; Ken Chant; Vision Publishing.

Worthies of England, The; The Folio Society, London, 1987.

Other Books by Ken & Alison Chant

Angelology
A study of the splendours of the heavenly realm

Attributes of Splendour
Reflections on the nature, being, and glory of God

Authenticity and Authority of the Bible
The Authenticity and Authority of scripture

Better then Revival
A Pragmatic look at Christian Ministry and the Idea of Revival

Building the Church God Wants
Not goal-setting, nor statistics, but faithfulness

Christian Life
A positive and creative approach to life.

Clothed with Power
A Pentecostal Theology of Holy Spirit baptism.

Corinthians
Studies in 1 Corinthians

Dazzling Secrets For Despondent Saints
The causes and the cure of depression.

Demonology
Understanding and overcoming our dark enemy

Discovery
Learning and living the will of God

Dynamic Christian Foundations
Studies in Foundational Christian Truths

Emmanuel 1
Jesus: Son of Man.

Emmanuel 2
Jesus: Man who is God.

Equipped
Understanding, receiving, & using the charismata to Serve

Faith Dynamics
The limitless power of faith in God

Great Words of the Gospel
The major themes of salvation and holiness.

Healing in the New Testament
The healing covenant now.

Healing in the Old Testament
The healing covenant then.

Highly Exalted
The ascension and heavenly ministry of Christ

Mountain Movers
Secrets of mountain-moving prayer

Royal Priesthood
The priesthood of all believers.

Songs to Live By
Studies in the Psalms and Christian worship.

Strong Reasons
The Bible & Science, and the Proofs of God.

The Cross and the Crown
The passion and resurrection of Christ.

The Pentecostal Pulpit
The art of preaching in the power of the Holy Spirit.

The World's Greatest Story
The dramatic first millennium of church history

Throne Rights
Our position and spiritual authority in Christ.

Understanding Your Bible
Studies in biblical hermeneutics.

Unsung Heroines

Sage counsel for women in leadership in the church.

When the Trumpet Sounds

Studies in the Return of Christ.

Walking In The Spirit

The Apostle Paul offers as the key to successful
Christian living the instruction "Walk in the Spirit"

www.ingramcontent.com/pod-product-compliance
Lightning Source LLC
Chambersburg PA
CBHW052010090426
42741CB00008B/1630